# Saved, Single & Frustrated

A Guide to Unleash the Best in You While You Wait

Indiana Tuggle

Victory
PUBLISHING INC

Copyright © 2015 by Indiana Tuggle

Victory Publishing Inc.

P.O. Box 752584

Memphis, TN 38175

All rights reserved. No part of this publication may be reproduced, stored in a retrieval system, or transmitted in any form or by any means – electronic, mechanical, photocopy, recording, or any other – except for brief quotations in printed reviews, without prior permission.

Scripture quotations marked NKJV are taken from the Holy Bible, New King James Version Copyright © 1979, 1980, 1982 by Thomas Nelson Inc. Scripture quotations marked AMP are taken from the Holy Bible, Amplified Version. Copyright © 1954, 1958, 1962, 1964, 1965, 1987 by The Lockman Foundation. Scripture quotations marked NLT are taken from New Living Translation (NLT) Holy Bible. New Living Translation copyright © 1996 by Tyndale Charitable Trust. Scripture quotations marked KJV are taken from King James Version.

Edited by: Zipporah Williams

ISBN 10: 0-9993411-2-4

ISBN 13: 978-0-9993411-2-4

Printed in the United States of America

# Acknowledgements

### To my Lord and Savior Jesus Christ

My, look how far we have come. Though the road has not always been easy, nor has it always been a joy, I can't complain. I understand the need for this journey and I am better, greater walking into my destiny. I know that as long as my eyes are stayed on you, the best is yet to come.

### To my friends, family, and loved ones

I am amazed at the amount of support you continue to give. Your encouragement is greatly appreciated.

# Dedication

This book is dedicated to single women all over the world who have become weary in well-doing and frustrated in the wait for their spouse. Stand and when you have done all else, stand therefore. God has not forgotten you. Have faith and confidence that your Mister is on the way. While you wait allow God to complete a work in you!

You are Blessed, and you are a Blessing to others!

# Table of Contents

Introduction .................................................................................................... 7

Chapter 1 Why Am I "Still" Single: Releasing the Frustration ................... 11

Chapter 2 You are Worthy: There is Nothing Wrong with You ................. 19

Chapter 3 Your Past Husbands: Breaking Soul Ties ................................... 29

Chapter 4 Christian Dating: Set the Standard and Stick to It .................... 41

Chapter 5 Dealing with Loneliness: If You Don't Like You, He Won't Either ..... 53

Chapter 6 Examine Yourself: Like Spirits Attract ....................................... 61

Chapter 7 Why Do You Want To Be Married? ............................................ 73

Chapter 8 Praying for Your Husband: The List ........................................... 83

Chapter 9 Preparing for Marriage ................................................................ 93

Chapter 10 A Closer Walk with Thee: Developing a Consistent Relationship with God .................................................................................................... 101

# INTRODUCTION

If you have read my first book, *Stop Asking Why Are You Single* then you have probably heard what I am about to say, perhaps more than once, but it bears repeating again:

*"Frustration is a result of trying to do something on your own that only God can do."*

Boy was I still frustrated! Let me catch you up. After the release of my first book a lot has happened. I will spare you the gory details (as I discuss them in full in the later chapters) and just give you the abbreviated version.

First, I got tired of waiting again, called my ex, thought he cared about me but just wasn't "the one" only to realize he was a complete DONKEY! (If you know what I mean) Next I was laid off of my job finding myself, Ms. Independent, unemployed for the first time EVER! Then, I officially started my own company and discovered it's not as easy as it seemed. I still was not making any money.

Desperate, lonely and frustrated, I cried out to the Lord for guidance and instruction. "Just write" he said. Excuse me? What do you mean just write? I have no job, no income, no one to help me, I could lose the house, and I could have to move back in with my mama! What do you mean just write? "I am your provider," he said "just write, I freed you up with this time."

The "Almost" encounter with my ex, left me grateful that I didn't have sex with him, yet still lonely in that I longed for companionship. Marriage was not as far from my mind as I thought it was. Yes, I received deliverance and healing from my past. Yes I had discovered my purpose and what I was meant to do, hence the starting of my own company, which kept me rather busy. But at the end of the day, I wanted someone to tell about my day, to worry about me getting in late, to hold me, to be vulnerable with. So again I asked God "Why am I STILL single."

I learned that discovering my purpose was to keep me busy doing God's work rather than wasting time on meaningless activities. But the love that I sought was only found in God. Have you ever longed for something so bad, yet feared that you wouldn't recognize it if it slapped you in the face wearing a "here I am" t-shirt with matching hat and stamp on the forehead? If what you wanted seemed like a fantasy or distant reality because you'd never seen it? Though you wanted it, your greatest fear was that you would mess it up?

My encounter with love was dysfunctional, and I knew it. The "love" that I knew and saw beat my mother, molested me, bullied me, incarcerated my brother, addicted my mother to drugs and alcohol, used me, abused me and left me with a trail of shame, regret, and unworthiness. The "love" I knew was a liar and did more harm than good. I needed to be reprogrammed.

*Saved, Single & Frustrated* answers the question of what to do while you wait. Single women are not just frustrated with not having a man. We are frustrated because it appears that sin is winning. Fornicators are happy. Adulterers are happy. Couples shacking and having children out of wedlock are happy. Pastors and men of standard in the church are choosing worldly women, who display their sinful lives on reality television, and are happy. Gold-diggers are happy. Or so that is what the enemy wants us to believe. He wants us to be frustrated when men and women cheat on their spouses. He wants us to be confused when unmarried men and women live and build lives together, calling marriage just a piece of paper. He wants us to be angry when "Single Life" is exemplified and glorified through promiscuous life styles. How is it that we who are living a holy and righteous life style as God intended seem to be last in receiving the marriage we desire?

*Saved, Single & Frustrated* will challenge single women to just S.T.O.P: **S**top asking why they are still single, **T**ake inventory of their own issues, **O**pen their hearts to the rod of correction, and **P**ray without ceasing. Stop asking friends and family to "hook them up" with a good guy. Stop trying to find a man. Stop asking other people, or reading magazine articles on how to get and keep a man. Stop seeking help from the created and go to the creator. God knows us better than we know ourselves. He knows what He requires for us to prepare for the marriage that He has for us. He required me to release the frustration, realize I am worthy, break soul ties, set standards in dating, deal with the loneliness, examine myself, check my motives in why I wanted to be married, pray for my future husband, prepare for marriage His way, and develop a consistent relationship with Him.

Though our preparation may be different, I hope that *Saved, Single & Frustrated* will encourage you to first seek God and then to do the work that is required. Once you do so you will have more confidence, as I do, that Mister is on the way. At the completion of this book, or shall I say this journey, I have a deeper revelation of who I am, who God is, and what is required for marriage....to be complete in Christ. Preparing for marriage is not about perfection or correcting all your faults, it's about being the best you for you, and above all it is about Love. Love began with God, was imparted in you, and must be given to others. Before we can truly love others we must first love ourselves unconditionally as God does. Let's get busy!

# Chapter 1
## Why Am I "Still" Single: Releasing the Frustration

*And let us not lose heart and grow weary and faint in acting nobly and doing right, for in due time and at the appointed season we shall reap, if we do not loosen and relax our courage and faint.*

Galatians 6:9 (AMP)

I'm a good girl. At least I think I am. I go to church every Sunday. I pay my tithes and offerings. Not only do I go to church, but I am not just a bench member, I am active. I am editor of the newsletter, leader of the Singles Ministry, and I even teach classes on occasion. Why Am I Still Single?

I really am a good girl. I messed up in the past, but I'm saving myself for marriage. I've been celibate over 6 years. Regardless of how many say I'm crazy or "Ain't nobody gonna wait till marriage to have sex," I resisted the urge, I do have urges, and I haven't burst. But how long must a sistah wait....Why Am I Still Single? I'm a good woman. I am educated. I have three degrees for Pete's sake. I own my own home, my car is paid for. Every piece of furniture is paid for. I have a good job, stable work history. I make my own money, pay my own bills, and travel on my on dime regularly. I put the "I" in independent. Why Am I Still Single?

I don't have any kids, no baby daddy drama. I ain't crazy, bitter, nor do I have a bad attitude….Well maybe sometimes. I'm a pretty cool chick. I'm cultured. I enjoy the arts, like to go to plays, and I can mingle in any crowd. My vocabulary is not limited to the latest slang or hip hop terms. I can hold a conversation on more than fashion, Hollywood who's who, the Housewives or Love and Hip Hop Atlanta, L.A., etc. I watch CNN. I like sports (Steeler Nation Baby!), or can at least pretend to for a couple of hours. Shopping is not my daily past-time. It's more like therapeutic release, only needed monthly. Scratch that last part…who am I kidding. But still Why Am I Still Single?

I'm a big, beautiful, woman, if I do say so myself. I have my own fashion; I know what looks good on me. Could I stand to lose a few pounds…Perhaps? Could I stand a break from my normal routine of work, home, work, home….Perhaps? I don't club, but I visit live music venues, restaurants, plays, movies, parks, malls, comedy clubs, etc. quite frequently. Homebody, Yes but I am no hermit. Why Am I Still Single?

I'm human. Sometimes I am tired of being alone. Sometimes I feel lonely. However, I have great friends and family. I am following my dreams. I have embarked on being a writer and a business owner. I have my head on straight. I examine my faults so I know I am not perfect but I know there is someone perfect for me out there. Why Am I Still Single?

Where is my Mr. Right? I'm sick and tired of the nothing brother. Ain't got nothing, don't want nothing, still living with his mama, baby mama drama having, back-child support paying or shall I say not paying, no car, no house, still holding on to childhood rap star dreams, can't hold a job for longer than six-months but yet want a sistah to have her stuff together kinda brotha. Ain't nobody got time for that! I'd rather stay single.

Where is my Mr. Right? I know he is out there. I am not naïve or angry to think that all men are dogs or there are no good men out there. I see him in my dreams. I hear about him in the media, portrayed in movies, read his letters to magazines or radio shows about his frustration to be all that he can be or his search for Ms. Right. He too is probably tired of the no good women who say they want a good man but find him and misuse and degrade him. How she keeps him from seeing his children, sleeps with his friends, spends all his money or only wants him for his money. I will wait for him.

Where is my Mr. Right? God promised me a husband. My God is not a liar. How long must I wait. Why has my time not come? I am ready to love and be loved. I am ready to build a family, to build memories, to share my life, to grow old together, to become one and yes to totally submit. I will wait for him.

I will not settle for Mr. Right now. I will not be blinded by the 6'2" frame, chocolate skin, bald head or muscular build. I will not be blinded by the BMW, Beamer, Benz, or whatever toy he uses to capture his prey. I will not be blinded by the million dollar mansion or bank account. I am not impressed with how good he says he is in bed. I am a woman of God, if you can't put a ring on it, you don't deserve my body. I will wait for better.

I will not settle for Mr. Right now. I will not be blinded by the smooth talk, swagger in his walk, or strength in his arms. I want more. I want commitment. I want true love. I will not settle for a temporary fix. I will not settle for partial loyalty, superficial clothing worn to mask a corroding spirit or evil intentions. I deserve better. I am better. I will wait for better.

Stop judging me. I am not jealous of you. You, ladies, who portray happiness behind "a man" who refuses to commit to you. Just because you been with him X amount of years does not constitute a relationship. News flash: being in a relationship does not mean you are not single. In fact you are just as single as I am because being unmarried makes you single. I don't covet your relationship!

Stop judging me. I don't need your advice. I don't need to wear more make-up, less clothing, or tighter clothing. I don't need to lose weight, gain weight, or dress in the latest fashion. I don't need to go to the club every weekend or drink myself into a drunken slumber to have a good time. I don't need to "give him something he can feel," especially so I can awaken the next day feeling worse than the day before. I don't covet your lifestyle!

Stop judging me. I am not lowering my standards. He must be a hard-working, God-fearing man of integrity who will love me unconditionally and not use me or abuse me mentally, physically, or emotionally. I will not settle for less. He cannot move in with me, drive my car, or have the milk without buying the cow. I don't want "any" man, I want the one God purposed for me.

Stop trying to change my mind. Married women, I still desire marriage. I understand marriage is hard work. I do not have delusions of grandeur, unrealistic expectations or the "happily ever after" syndrome. I know your marriage is rocky right now, and I continue to pray for you. I am not easily persuaded.

Stop trying to change my mind. Stop speaking negativity over my marriage because yours is not working out. I get it. You think you chose the wrong one. He changed, or didn't change, after the wedding. He doesn't understand you and you don't understand him. He cheated. You cheated. The kids are the only thing holding you together. I know it's not a fairytale. Better yet I know your story is not the story for all marriages. I still pray for you, but I am not easily persuaded.

Stop trying to hit on me, married men. When did "I'm not seeing anyone" become a sign of desperation? Or an invitation to accept your infidelity and willingness to become the "other" woman or "side chick." I don't want you. I don't date married men. I will not partake in hurting or disrespecting my sister. You reap what you sow. I will not sow that adultery into my marriage.

Stop trying to hit on me, married men. I am not a fool. I know all you want is sex. You ain't that fine to risk going to hell for. Why would I settle for part-time love or a few minutes of lust? I want my own relationship, my own husband. I respect all marriages and hope that the next woman will do the same for me. If you don't value your commitment, why would I think it would be different with me? If you would cheat on her with me, what makes me think you will be faithful to me? Been there done that, bought the t-shirt and the hat, not going down that road or even in that direction again.

Stop hitting on me, married men. Separated is not the new single. You are still married. If she was that bad, why have you not gotten a divorce? If finances are keeping you with her, you don't have enough money to be head of my household over here. Close one chapter before you start another one.

Dead beat fathers, please keep it moving. If you can't pay child support or spend quality time with your children, how can you portray "man of the year" to me? If you can't take care of your flesh and blood, you certainly can't take care of me. If you still blaming the mother of your children, kick rocks, a grown man takes responsibility for his actions. Baby mama drama ain't cute. Work that out before you attempt to bring somebody else into your life.

Players play on. But I have the right to decide if I want to be part of the game. Games are for children. Mature adults, grown folks, don't got time for games. AIDS and STDs are real. Domestic violence is real. Stalking is real. Death at the hands of a loved one is real. You can't continue to play with people's hearts and expect to walk away at your leisure. I don't want to be the innocent victim of your ex nor do I want to be the ex, now incarcerated because you can't keep it in your pants. If you want to play the field, be honest, I won't judge, but I won't be your next victim either. Keep it moving.

The true definition of single is unmarried. Point blank period. Long term relationship, boo'd up, dating, etc. does not mean you are not single. Without a ring and that "piece of paper" you say don't matter, you are still single. I don't want to accept "any" man just to keep from being alone. I would rather wait for "the" man that God has designed just for me. Singles do not just desire a relationship, we want marriage. Yes we know that dating and relationships have to precede marriage but marriage is the ultimate goal. Therefore we chose not to waste our time with those who are not like minded.

I think I got it all out. Please don't confuse frustration for anger. I am not angry. At least I don't think I am. As singles, we are tired of people trying to define who we are, what makes us happy or who should make us happy. We also get tired of being stigmatized and devalued. Yes I know self-worth comes from within. But we should not have to prove or defend our happiness or current situation. We are human and our moments of loneliness or desire to have a mate, in which we chose to voice it, should not be met with discussions of you need to do this and that. This and that is dependent upon several scenarios and therefore one suggestion, or your suggestion, may not be best.

Frustration comes from constantly trying to or having to explain why we are single. What is it that you want us to say? What answer will appease your curiosity? Are you expecting a list of inadequacies or mistakes of the past? Do you want us to profess to you why dating us is such a bad idea? The same reason you are in a relationship is the same reason we are not in one. God decided it was best at this appointed time. The beauty of singleness is not in the freedom to date whomever, though that is a bonus. But the beauty of singleness is the freedom to do the will of the Lord without having to consult with a spouse.

## **Why Am I "Still" Single**

Only God can answer this question. His answer may surprise you. God does not look at the outer as man does. So the answer is not in the physical. Stop allowing your married or coupled friends to tell you what you are not or what you should do to get a mate. You are not ugly, too fat, too thin, too crazy, too mean, too un/educated, too smart, too intimidating, have too high standards, or whatever the world, past relationships, yourself, or even what your friends have told you are the reasons for your singleness.

Every blessing from God comes with an appointed time. If the time for your marital bliss has not come, then only God can say why. Are there things about you that may need changing? Perhaps. But I can guarantee it has to do with matters of the heart rather than your outer appearance. Get in the word and allow God to show you who you are.

If it still angers or frustrates you to be asked this question, then it is because you are not happy. Your frustration is written all over your face. Then you go out into the world and the enemy throws it back to you to fan the flames. Happiness is awaiting you now. It does not begin when you get a man.

Stop questioning God. You are exactly where He wants you to be. In the meantime, while you wait He has need of you. Your gifts are required in the kingdom. The world is waiting on you. Stop worrying about what you don't have. Blessings await you now.

Only God can complete you. Only God can provide happiness. Only God can provide companionship. Only God can show you true intimacy. God is our everything. Lay your fears, concerns, worries, at His feet. Stop focusing on the when and why and just expect the promise.

*And the Lord God said, "It is not good that man should be alone; I will make him a helper comparable to him." – Genesis 2: 18 (NKJV)*

We know that it is not God's desire for us to be alone. Therefore it is natural to desire a mate. But the key phrase is "And the Lord God said." God decided it was not good for man to be alone. God decided He would make him a helper comparable to him. God decided to make woman from his rib and presented her to him. Adam did not know he was alone. Adam did not desire a mate. Nowhere does it mention that Adam was complaining about being in the garden alone. In fact, Adam was doing what God told him to do: tending and keeping the garden, naming the animals, enjoying all the fruits, etc. Also, when Eve was presented to Adam, the first thing he did was "name" her.

*If you abide in Me, and My words abide in you, you will ask what you desire, and it shall be done for you. – John 15:7 (NKJV)*

God's timing is not our timing. If we are honest, our desire for a mate is based on fleshly desires and lust. Allow God to complete a work in you. Allow His will and desire for your life to become your will and desire. At the appointed time, God will provide your mate. Until then, grow closer in relationship in Him and pursue the purpose He created you for.

# Chapter 2
## You are Worthy:
### There is Nothing Wrong with You

*Blessed be the God and Father of our Lord Jesus Christ, who has blessed us with every spiritual blessing in the heavenly places in Christ, just as He chose us in Him before the foundation of the world, that we should be holy without blame before Him in love, having predestined us to adoption as sons by Jesus Christ to Himself, according to the good pleasure of His will, to the praise of the glory of His grace by which He made us accepted in the Beloved.*

*Ephesians 1: 3–6 (NKJV)*

Fat, Black, A\*\*!

Hey Kool-Aid!

Big Baby!

Fat, Ugly Tail

I could go on and on. How could kids be so cruel? How can one go from Momma's "pretty, fat, chocolate baby" and Daddy's 'Baby Girl" to Fat this, fat that, big this, big that, ugly this, black that all in one day?

They are stupid kids, they don't know any better. Sure, but the words still hurt. Knowing this still didn't make the sting less painful. If it only happened as a child, perhaps I could have healed before adulthood. But it continued. Each new school presented a new bully or a new mean girl. Why did they hate me so much, I wondered? Why didn't they like me, I questioned. By the time I went to high school, I was tired of arguing, tired of fighting, and just internalized it all.

Some might say, "That was years ago!" Perhaps, but when you experience failed relationship, after failed relationship, you ponder whether any of it is true. Singleness has a way of digging up the hurt. The enemy seems to rehash the right baggage or negativity at the opportune time. Why is it that we can remember the negative, vividly in living color, as if it happened yesterday? But the good things, we have a hard time remembering or forget the details. Simple, why would the devil want you to think happy thoughts?

The longer one is single, the more time we spend alone with our thoughts, the longer we feel isolated and punished. If the enemy can keep you in a state of isolation, he is able to keep you from true happiness. Life happens but at some point you have to tell yourself "Get over it." Understand that it is a trick of the enemy. His job is that you don't know who you are. His goal is to use your past, your thoughts, and your emotions against you.

*Lest Satan should take advantage of us, for we are not ignorant of his devices – 2 Corinthians 2:11 (NKJV)*

Now that you know it is him. Fight through! Fight to keep going. Fight not to give up. As you listen to the voice of God, as you do His will, the voice of the enemy will get weaker.

Are you not worth it? Recognize you are worth the better life you desire. You are worth the wait. To wait does not mean to be still and do nothing. Doing nothing gives the enemy victory. Be patient with yourself. Overlooking the negativity, learning to see past the negative words spoken over you, learning to live with no regret, no shame, or no sense of rejection takes time.

Do you believe you are worth it? I hear many singles, including myself, say the infamous phrase "I'm worth the wait." Do you really believe you are worth the wait? Are you worth forgiving yourself and letting go of the past? Are you worth realizing you possess inner and outer beauty? Are you worth uncovering the real you behind the smile, great hair, designer clothes, etc.? Are you worth becoming the best you, the woman of your spouse's dreams? Time is not standing still. As you go, as you fight, as you trust God, you are getting stronger.

When the enemy says "No," keep fighting, God says "Yes."

When the enemy says "You're ugly," keep fighting, God calls you beautiful.

When the enemy says "You're fat or too thin," keep fighting, God says "You are his masterpiece."

When the enemy says, "No one cares," keep fighting, God cares and others do too.

You are worth the wait. Don't allow the enemy to cause you to doubt who you are. You are made in God's image. You are His mouthpiece. You speak and hear from the mouth of God. Keep going. Don't stop. Don't slow down. Doing so can cause you to miss God's hand and thus delay the wait.

You are worth the wait. God came to give you life. Anything that diminishes that life is not God. You quiet the enemy with the word. Keep praying, studying, and communing with God. You know His voice, don't doubt what you hear.

*My sheep hear My voice, and I know them and they follow Me. And I give them eternal life, and they shall never perish; neither shall anyone snatch them out of My hand. - John 10: 27 – 28 (NKJV)*

Giving up is not an option. Forgetting is not an option. Obedience moves God. Obedience causes the hand of God to pour out blessings. God cannot order your steps if you do not seek His face. It is a trick of the enemy that causes you to stop reading the word and/or to stop praying. God deserves more than a quick "Thank you Lord" when you wake up in the morning. Or a speedy prayer to "Watch over you and your family" as you drive in for work. Purposely make time for Him and He will pause time for you. Lack of prayer life causes confusion and the ease to become overwhelmed at life. God does not speak without the word. Constant communication is needed to build a sustainable relationship with God.

Without a personal relationship with God. We become dependent on others. Calling friends, church mothers, ministers, pastors, etc. asking for prayer. Going to prophetic worship services, seeking a word from the Lord. Yes we need each other, and need others to pray for us. But the same way God speaks to them, and through them, He can speak in and through you. It's time to become big little Christians and seek God for ourselves. What if that person has an off day? We are all human. What if they forget to pray or are not under the anointing and tell you something wrong. Are you going to leave your fate in someone else's hand?

Life happens to us all. Things come that bend us or even knock us off our feet. Sunday morning service or weekly bible studies are great, but it is what you do the rest of the week that will sustain you or enable you to stand during the storm. If we examine ourselves we will find that we have more time than we think. The time spent watching TV, or on social media could be used to commune with the Lord. Is it really productive to discuss the happening of every new show, respond to every post on Facebook or just spend an hour or two scrolling, or uploading videos or pictures on Instagram or Twitter? We cannot fill our time with junk and expect good fruit to produce in times of trouble.

You are worth the wait. God's ways are not hidden. His plan for your life is not hidden. He is faithful even when you are not. But your lack of communing causes His hand to be slothful. Remember you are not waiting on God. The wait is for you. He is waiting on you. The wait produces patience, trust, removes impurities, and strengthens the spiritual man. What you do during the wait, determines the length of time you must wait.

If you do nothing, you must wait until you do something.

If you say nothing, you must wait until you speak.

If you stand still, you must wait until you move.

God's hand is not still concerning you, you are standing still.

As you go, God goes also!

As you do, God does also!

As you speak, God speaks also.

We are God in the Earth, He cannot move in your life without you!

To say "I don't know what to do," is also a trick of the enemy. You know His voice. The enemy speaks to your past, that's all he has access to. God speaks to your Now. He is not in your future trying to pull you through. He is with you now. Harken His voice and do what is required.

*Can two walk together, unless they are agreed? - Amos 3:3 (NKJV)*

God is with you. God is in you. The enemy is on the outside. He brings up the past (keeps you doing what is comfortable). Again God speaks to your now, commanding you to do what you have never done. Procrastination will cause you to miss your blessing. The world is waiting for you. Your spouse is waiting for you. The enemy tries to pull you backward, God is moving you forward.

One of the difficulties in singleness is found in the constant worrying about "when" the meeting between you and your spouse will happen. I wondered what he would look like. Where it would happen. If I would recognize him. Have I already met him and scared him off. Is he someone I already know? Then the fear comes in. Fear of messing up. Fear of being alone. Fear of wondering will I ever be "good" enough for him. I am not perfect. I am spoiled and selfish at times. I have been hurt many times and it caused me to put up a wall. I am also vulnerable which causes me to seek love from others and act without thinking. I struggle with loneliness which causes me to seek companionship in online dating or with guys I know I cannot see a future with. Singleness causes one to doubt themselves, their beauty, their abilities, their "goodness", their self-worth. We wonder whether our standards are too high, which is why we are not dating. Or too low, which is why we keep meeting the wrong one.

Two years ago I started dating this guy. Everything in me said run. When I looked at him, I literally saw the face of the devil. He had tried to date me in the past but it didn't work out. Then I was in school, spent a lot of time studying and working, and he seemed too controlling wanting all my time and always questioning my activities. Plus he lived with his mom, had no car, nor a job. But at this time, I was lonely. I was feeling rejected because I met a guy online and thought he was a good candidate to start a relationship with. I even went to Chicago to see him and I thought we had a good time. We had a close encounter in the hotel, a little touchy feely, but I remained good and did not break my vow of celibacy. After I got back home, the guy texted me that he didn't want to do a long distance relationship, and couldn't handle the thought of not being able to see his girlfriend daily. I was devastated, hurt, and felt deceived. Later I wondered was it because I didn't have sex with him? As time went on I found out he actually began to date someone in my hometown of Memphis. After that I was really lonely and when this nothing-brother tried again. I agreed to go out with him.

I should have run on the first date. I had to go pick him up! But we went out anyway. From that day we were inseparable. He texted me all day while I was at work. I left work and went straight to his mom's house to pick him up. I was in class one night a week, but as soon as it was over, to his house I went. We even went out a few nights a week. I was enjoying his company. We talked about our dreams. We discussed the Word, or at least tried to. He said I played the antagonist to everything he said. My problem was, he generally tried to tell me what theologians said and what the scripture meant back in that day. While I was going off revelation from the Holy Spirit regarding what I was going through or had been through. But hey at least we discussed the Word. He was supposedly a man of God, called to be an Apostle.

One day we were at my house, watching a movie. Sitting close, cuddling on the couch, led to kissing, touching, and him performing oral sex on me. But hey, we didn't go all the way. Two days later, we were in my room, watching a moving, cuddling, kissing, touching, and this time we went all the way. It lasted all of five minutes. I pushed him off me, ran in the bathroom and began crying like a baby. Six years of celibacy, six years of waiting for Mr. Right down the drain. He came in the bathroom to console me. I put my clothes on and took him home. We stood in his drive way, prayed, repented, and promised not to do it again. He wanted more than sex, I was his wife, he said, he knew it when he first met me. Yeah right. Three days later we did it again...and again...and again. Before you know it, he had moved in, was dropping me off at work in my car, and using my car to do odd carpentry jobs. What happened? We started planning a life. He told me about the thousands of dollars he was behind in child support. I didn't care, we all have debt, my student loan is a bugger bear. He told me how his baby momma doesn't let him see the kids much, so I never met them. He told me he was building his carpentry business, so he wouldn't be able to help with the bills. God told him he was called to be an Apostle, so as he did the work of the Lord, God would take care of his family. But what about the man being the head? What about "a man who don't work don't eat." What about, "you must think I'm a fool!"

I have been Ms. Independent all my life. Been working since I was 16. Moved out my mom's house at 19 and haven't been back since. I worked hard, went to school earned my degrees, bought my own house, paid off my own car....I must be a fool! How could I allow someone to come into my life, partake in all the blessings God has given me, without bringing something to the table? As we started planning a wedding, I started having headaches, panic attacks etc. My friends were having interventions with me.... "But I am in love," I said. Truth is I felt like I had already slept with him, so why not marry him. But what really got me was when dude said, "He was not a provider", and "that I should be ok with paying the bills, as long as I knew he was focused on the business." Did I forget to mention, there would be no business, if it weren't for me. I made flyers for him, I made him drive around and put them in people's mail box. I allowed him to use my car to go to the job sites. I was committed to helping him, and all he was willing to do is let me take care of him. What was I thinking? I knew this was wrong, I knew he was the wrong one, but I was lonely and I was tired of waiting.

One day I went to church, while he stayed at my house, because he didn't like my church. My pastor gave me a word from the Lord that knocked me off my feet. He told me the guy was not my husband, a relationship was not supposed to be that hard, and deep inside I already knew. Truth is I was tired of being alone. Six years of celibacy is easy when you are not dating anyone. I dated that guy for three months and was ready to marry him, not because he was Mr. Wonderful and swept me off my feet, but because I was lonely.

It's been two years since that fiasco and I have just now forgiven myself. I wondered how I could be so vulnerable. How could I allow someone, who I knew wasn't right, come in and mess up my preparation for my husband. How could I be so smart, educated, etc., yet make such a stupid mistake. Condemnation does not come from God. It is a device from the enemy to keep us wallowing in regret and shame. Boy was I ashamed. The worst part was I had given him my body, I broke my vow with the Lord.

I soon learned that he was a test. First I learned that I had to be delivered from loneliness. I discovered that loneliness is not something that is taken away in one day. It is a daily fight. I am human, so yes I will desire the company of a man. But it is what loneliness makes me do, that I needed to address. Loneliness made me seek love and attention on the internet and from guys who I knew where not best for me. Second, I learned that celibacy is not something you do to prove worthy of the blessings of God, it is an expression of your love for Him and desire to keep His commandments. Those first six years, were not punishment, God protected me from myself and He is still protecting me now.

Lastly, I learned I am worth the wait. I am worth the wait for my deliverance. I am worth the wait for my abundant life. I am worth the wait to recognize my own beauty, inside and out. I am worth the wait to be free from the opinion and approval seeking of others. I am worth the wait to enjoy my own company. I am worth the wait to find the joy in being alone but not lonely. There is nothing wrong with me. The pains of my past have distorted my view of myself. I am worth the wait for clear vision. God promised me beauty for ashes. I don't know when Mr. Right is coming or where we will meet. But I know he is coming, because My God is not a liar.

During the wait I have discovered who I am. I am a giver. I give love through gifts and time. I receive love through words of encouragement, affirmation, and quality time. My purpose is to help others discover their purpose. I am transparent and my transparency draws people to me. It was a trick of the enemy telling me I was being used. The people were not using me. They needed me, to guide them, to encourage them, to help them become better. But because I didn't know who I was, the enemy sent users, abusers, to prevent me from discovering my gift. But God promised me that my latter days would be better. God is drawing people to me. People who need my heart, my compassion, and are not concerned with my size, my clothes, my hair, etc.

Our worth is not determined by what we did, who we dated, what we have, or what we don't have. Our worth is determined by God.

*Before I formed you in the womb I knew you; before you were born I sanctified you; I ordained you a prophet to the nations. - Jeremiah 1:5 (NKJV)*

Because He knew us, our life, our past, our mistakes are not a surprise, nor did they make Him change his mind concerning us. You are worthy because He who lives in you called you worthy. You are worth any amount of time it may take to obtain the fullness of God's love and plan for your life. What if he is in the journey? If you never start, you will never meet. You are worth the journey. If God gave us what we wanted when we wanted, we probably wouldn't appreciate it. The blessings of God draw us closer to Him, not distract us from Him. If he is a distraction, taking you from church, from the word, from prayer, he is not from God.

God must restore order. Put Him first and everything else will fall in line. If He is not first, second, third, and forth are out of order as well. You are worth the restoration.

God is time. Time will not run out before his promises come to fruition in your life.

*God is not a man that He should lie. Nor a son of man, that He should repent. Has He said, and will He not do? Or has He spoken, and will He not make it good?*
*- Numbers 23:19 (NKJV)*

You are worth the time. God is not mocked. The righteous will not be forsaken. Your good is not forgotten. He has not taken a blind eye to your efforts. You are worth the sacrifice.

# Chapter 3
## Your Past Husbands: Breaking Soul Ties

*They say, "if a man divorces his wife, and she goes from him and becomes another man's, may he return to her again?' Would not that land be greatly polluted? But you have played the harlot with many lovers; yet return to Me," says the Lord.*
*Jeremiah 3:1 (NKJV)*

*You will never find another one like me.*
*I will never love anyone the way I love you.*
*I will love you forever.*
*I promise I will never hurt you.*
*I promise I will never leave you.*

I'm sure we have all heard our share of "I promise" and "I will never" to last, if not a lifetime, at least a decade. Get over it, they say.

Singleness brings about many emotions. Its highs make you feel you can conquer the world. But its lows take you to a place of darkness you never knew existed and would be ashamed if others knew. Mr. Wrong can seem so right while you're in your pit.

I just want someone to talk to, we can be friends. The safety of his arms. The warmth of his touch. His attention to detail. The whispering of sweet nothings. The passion in his eyes. Your body still tingles when you think of his touch.

Why not call him. (Don't do it)

I just need to be in the presence of a man. (Don't do it)

Your body longs for him, but your mind is screaming "Run Forest, Run!"

I just want to talk. I need to *feel* loved. (But I love you more!)

You call anyway. The conversation led to a movie, the movie led to sitting in a dark car with his lips and hands all over you.

Must break away….. But it feels so good. (Don't do it)

You break away and head home. More late night conversations, lead to dinner, lead to him in your house on the same couch, cuddling in the same position, on your back, legs high, (this is not right) but the pleasure of his tongue has persuaded you otherwise.

Stop, we can't, we're supposed to be friends. I can't do this. But I still love you, you are still my wife. I have always loved you. As you slowly melt into his arms. (But I love you more!)

You got to go, I need time to think. He finally leaves. You scream a sigh of relief. If he was wrong before, why is he so right now?

A good night's sleep is all you need. Why did you call him? Why did you give in to the flesh? You knew what would happen. You knew what could happen. If you play with fire you will surely get burned. Do you really think you can be friends with someone you have been intimate with? Do you really feel Mr. Wrong would make a good friend? You opened the door, so you have to close it.

I'll just ignore his call and he will get the picture. You can run but you can't hide. Wait, I got it, I will send him a text. "I'm sorry for contacting you, it was a mistake, we can't be friends, and there is too much history."

But you didn't anticipate his response: "I don't like you anyway, you've been used so much that you have become the user. You need psychiatric help. You are not fit to help anybody and you call yourself a counselor. I will write a letter to your church and tell them you're not fit to be over a singles ministry. You too fat for me anyway. Nobody will ever love you, you don't even love yourself." Wow, now there is the Mr. Wrong I walked away from, welcome back. Now I remember why we didn't work. Are you surprised when the snake bit you?

What just happened here? Why is he so mad? When I called him, I specifically said I wanted to be friends and needed someone to talk to. Did he have his own agenda? Was he hoping we would reconnect? How could he love me one minute, and hate me the next. I don't have time, nor do I want to ride this rollercoaster anymore. I can't believe I risked how far I've come for a few minutes of self-gratification. Why did I look back? Mr. Wrong is still Mr. Wrong.

Ever wonder why that trip down memory lane, never includes the hurt, confusion, or drama that you went through. At least that first look over your shoulder doesn't. It's not until you turn all way around, that you remember the pain.

**You must sever the ties of your past before you can move on!**

I forgave him, you say. I forgave myself, you say. So why do you continue to take two steps forward, only to take one step back?

"There is something that you find difficult to give up somewhere in your life. Anything you allow to continue in your life becomes bond. The deeper the bond, the harder to release it. You don't know how tied you are until you get ready to give it up. You can become bonded to something that contradicts your destiny and eventually you will be required to give it up."
– T.D. Jakes

God wants to break the cycle of being in and out of bad relationships. The cycle of being in and out of this Christian walk. You have to get to a point where you no longer settle for the counterfeit and are willing to wait for the promise.

We will get into how to break soul ties later, but first let's get into how to identify soul ties. Some of you may be confused. Just because you have "moved on" does not mean the soul tie is broken.

## How do you identify soul ties?

***He constantly pulls you away from your destiny.***

This can be confusing because we all long for relationship or quality time with a person or doing something we enjoy doing. But if it distracts you from what God called you to do or limits your time to do what God would have you to do then it is a soul tie. If all of a sudden you are with this person and you stop going to church, stop praying, stop meditating and stop spending time with God. He is not the one. This goes for activities as well. If all your spare time is spent doing this activity and you don't have time to pray, study or read the word. It has to go.

*You shall have no other gods before Me. - Exodus 20:3 (NKJV)*

You have made that thing or that person your god. Generally it's sudden at first. He is taking you out, you enjoy spending time with him and getting to know him. Nothing wrong with that, right? Wrong. Why would God send you someone who distracts you or takes you away from Him? Remember God speaks in and through His word. If you have stopped your time with God, how will you hear the Holy Spirit when and if He says "Walk Away?" Godly soul ties draw you closer to Him, draw you closer to your purpose. There must be balance.

Let's revisit the guy I was talking about earlier. When we first started dating, we would talk on the phone for hours, all night even. He texted me all day while I was at work. When I left work, we hooked up, went out for dinner, and talked on the phone all night afterwards till 4 and 5 o'clock in the morning. Even when I started school, I could not study because he wanted to be with me and I wanted to be with him. On occasion I would say, "I need to study today so I will see you tomorrow." He would respond, "You can study with me there." I would give in and go pick him up. My spare time was taken. Not only did I not have time for God, I didn't have time for me!

### He constantly disrupts your peace

Confusion is not from God. If the statement "I'm confused" ever comes out your mouth, that is your first clue to run, Forest run! God's purpose and plan for our lives is clear. Confusion is a sign that you have walked away from God.

*For He [Who is the source of their prophesying] is not a God of confusion and disorder but of peace and order. As [is the practice] in all the churches of the saints (God's people), - 1 Corinthians 14:33 (AMP)*

There is no confusion in the word. If you are praying and reading as you should, you would not be confused. Confusion is a result of conflicting priorities and conflicting agendas. Confusion is a sign of internal conflict. Your flesh and spirit are fighting. Your flesh has taken over and the spirit is fighting to regain control. You can't sleep and you are restless, tossing and turning all night. You begin to have weird dreams. Headaches and migraines take over. Your thoughts are jumbled, all over the place. That wrinkle in your forehead becomes more noticeable and permanent. You start to feel something is not right, but your body is enjoying it. You are having fun, you say, but your spirit is in a state of unrest.

### Anger

When you are in denial and are asked to give something up, anger is the first sign that should let you know you are in trouble. In essence, what is going on is your flesh is having a temper tantrum. Like a little child, you are mad that you can't have what you want.

*Pride goes before destruction, and a haughty spirit before a fall. - Proverbs 16:18 (AMP)*

Because the Holy Spirit lives in us, He loves us, His job is to lead us into all truths. He will warn us before we mess up. The warning is almost always internal first. That small still voice that says "Don't go," "Don't do," or my personal favorite "But I love you more." If we ignore the internal warning, He may send it through a friend or family member. It is not a coincidence that all of a sudden a friend, church member, co-worker, etc out the blue asks you "Is everything ok" or "who's the new fella in your life." While you may answer "fine" or "none of your business," the question was intended to provoke thought and self-examination of your actions.

I remember when I was dating Mr. Wrong. All my co-workers watched me, laughing and snickering on the phone, him dropping me off at work in my car, and me strutting around as if I were on cloud 9. The minute I opened my mouth and said "we're getting married," one by one, they came to me and let me know how they felt. "Do you really think he is God's best for you?" I became defensive and proclaimed to be happy and in love. But I laid awake at night wondering if I was making a mistake. I knew he was wrong the moment I started dating him, but I settled. I wanted to feel loved, I wanted to spend time with someone, and I was tired of being alone. But the God we serve will not allow us to sell our birthright for temporary gratification!

## How do you break soul ties?

### Discover the root of the problem

Go into the deep. I'm sure you already know why Mr. Wrong was wrong. But he seemed right at first! What did he give you? That false sense of receiving what you thought you needed or what you thought was priority is the key to discover why you chose him, why you stayed with him, and why you keep going back. Maybe you don't go back to him (one particular person) but it's the same devil, different face, and different name.

I thought sexual molestations was the root of my problems. But I can truly say I am over that. As I went deeper, I examined what each man in my past gave me. There was a reoccurring theme: "the desire to be loved, needed, wanted, and to be told I was beautiful." So what if I had to give sex, endure infidelity, or struggle financially to get it. So what if I still felt empty and wanted more than they could give. When did I stop feeling loved, needed or wanted? Why did I need to be told I was beautiful? Why didn't I know I was beautiful?

Ask God to take you to the place of the wound. There you will find the answer to why you do the things that you do. That place of vulnerability creates an entrance to ungodly soul ties. In our quest to self-medicate, to heal the wound, we put pressure on people or things who are unable to give you what you need. They serve as temporary relief. We create a cycle, and each time the cycle repeats, it's like snatching the Band-Aid off over and over.

*Beware lest anyone cheat you through philosophy and empty deceit, according to the tradition of men, according to the basic principles of the world, and not according to Christ. For in Him dwells all the fullness of the Godhead bodily; and you are complete in Him, who is the head of all principality and power. – Colossians 2: 8 – 10 (NKJV)*

Relationships are meant to *compliment* both parties, not *complete*. Only God can complete you. We all know the story of Jacob, Leah and Rachel. Leah had a Spirit of Rejection. Her father didn't value her, he called her ugly, and she was given to Jacob in deception. She attempts to fix in her adulthood what went wrong in her childhood. Again where there is a wound or injury, that place of vulnerability, creates an opening for the enemy to create a soul tie. God saw that Leah was unloved and opened her womb. Each time she had a child, Reuben, Simeon, and Levi, she was hoping that her husband would love her. But it was not until she bore Judah that she said "Now will I praise the Lord." (Genesis 29: 31-35)

As Paula White explained, sometimes we can take a blessing from the Lord and use it to gain attention and affection from others, when all the time God is saying "But I love you more!" As a child I wanted my mother's attention more than anything. But she was addicted to drugs and alcohol and spent most of her time with her friends. Don't get me wrong, she was what I called a "functioning drug addict." She always made sure my brother and I had a roof over our head, clothes on our back and food to eat. But physically she was not there. I remember coming home from school. She would cook dinner and then leave. When she returned home, we would be asleep. I did everything to get her attention, I was a good student and made A's and B's all through grade school and even high school. But it wasn't enough. I was a sensitive child, didn't take a lot of spankings to keep me in order. Instead, the yelling and name calling kept me in my place. But soon, that grew into anger and resentment. I sought after men to love me, to value me, to tell me I was beautiful. I like Leah, developed a spirit of rejection and abandonment in an attempt to fix in my adulthood what went wrong in my childhood.

### *Identify and acknowledge the lie*

The time has come for you stop burying your hurt. Burying is an act of shame. When you are ashamed of what happened, to prevent others from finding out, you bury it. But remember a seed planted in the ground, when watered, will bear fruit. How did you water it? By self-medicating. And by doing so, the fruits of dysfunction, un-forgiveness, anger, etc have taken root. First identify the lie and what it made you do. I believed my mother didn't love me, and food became my comfort. Sometimes what we use to fix it or how we fix it, creates more damage. Food caused me to become overweight. Seeking love from men, led to fornication and a series of failed relationships. Next, acknowledge that the medication is not working. Food is not my friend and no man can love me if I don't love myself.

*The thief cometh not, but for to steal, and to kill, and to destroy: I am come that they might have life, and that they might have it more abundantly. - John 10:10 (KJV)*

The enemy launched an attack to steal your identity, kill your dreams, and destroy your future. But God wants to heal the wound so that you may have abundant life. Realize it wasn't about you, but rather it was about who you were. Recognize that though the pain seemed to last a lifetime, it did not kill you. You should be dead. But God said no. The lie is that you cannot recover. The lie is that you are not valuable. The lie is that you are not worthy. The lie is that you are incapable of love. The lie is that you are ugly. The longer you believe the lie, the longer you sit in darkness.

**Release the hurt**

This is one of the stages of forgiveness I spoke about in *Stop Asking Why Are You Single."* It is not enough to say I forgive you. If you are still hurting, no matter how many times you say I forgive you, your body is not responding because it does not know what to do with the hurt. Find a healthy way for you to release the hurt. Talk to a counselor, psychologist, or your pastor. Go to the person. This one is tricky. We can control ourselves but we cannot control the other person. You may not be ready for their response. So I suggest that you pray and ask God for guidance. If the person is unavailable or has passed on, write a letter. Writing a letter is also beneficial if you don't want to talk to the person face to face.

I wrote a letter to both my mother and my biological father, for the same reason. They are both still living and I could talk to them in person. However I wanted to release and move on. The child in me needed to be heard, but the adult in me, was ready to forgive and build a new relationship from this moment forward. Now, the conversation I want to have with them both is twofold. First, I need to apologize. I need to apologize to my mother for not always honoring her with my words. My anger led me to talk to her in rudeness and to say "no" when I could have said "yes" to some things she asked or wanted me to do. I need to apologize to my father for not allowing him to be who he is and holding him to a standard of who I thought he should be.

Next, I want a discussion of expectations and how to move forward. With my mom it is a matter of respecting me as an adult and accepting me as I am. My love languages are words of affirmation and quality time. But when I don't do what she wants when she wants, she talks down to me, which always hurts my feelings. My father is similar, he will say he will do this and that, or that he will come over to spend time with me, and he doesn't. So generally I avoid his calls and don't call him.

*Honor thy father and thy mother: that thy days may be long upon the land which the Lord thy God giveth thee. - Exodus 20:12 (KJV)*
*A new commandment I give unto you, that ye love one another; as I have loved you, that ye also love one another. By this shall all men know that ye are my disciples, if ye have love one to another - John 13: 34-35 (KJV)*

When we are hurting we are incapable of receiving and giving love. As God's people, we bear witness of Him. We represent Christ. We cannot preach salvation, with a heart of hate, bitterness, un-forgiveness, pride, etc. When we are hurting we are unable to be used by God and by default are being used by the enemy. By releasing the hurt, we invite love in, and we invite the Spirit of God into His rightful resting place.

**Stop going back.**
Stop trying to pull back what is no longer a part of your life. God is not going to break the soul tie for you. You must do it! We know the story of Abraham, Sarah and Hagar. Once Sarah bore Isaac, she saw Isaac being

mocked by Ishmael and asked Abraham to put Ismael and his mother Hagar out. Abraham was grieved, as this was his son and bondwoman (Hagar was a soul-tie). But God spoke to Abraham and told him to do as Sarah said, as the promise was in Isaac, however He would make a great nation out of Ishmael as well. Sarah could have put her out. God could have spoken to Hagar and told her to leave. But it was Abraham who had to do it.

You have to do it. If God takes it away, it's not a sacrifice, and God gets no glory. The ultimate sacrifice of praise is the denial of flesh. Anytime you deny your flesh and say "God, I love you more," you give the sacrifice of praise. God will give you the strength and power to walk away. We just have to look for it. The revelation of truth, will set you free.

*And ye shall know the truth, and the truth shall make you free. - John 8:32 (KJV)*

Love is blind. What this statement means is that love can prevent you from seeing the truth. I remember I dated this guy for 4 years. We were living together. He was married but "separated" when we met. However, he still had not filed for divorce, though he claimed to love me and wanted to marry me. I was trying to help the man get a divorce. I was helping him find a lawyer, and was even willing to help him pay for it. One day, it hit me: "Indiana, you really expect the Lord to bless you with someone else's husband?" So I got up the courage to tell him that I couldn't continue to live in sin and expect the Lord to be pleased. Over the course of a year, he would come to my house at least once a month asking me to take him back. At first, yell at him, asking him why he kept popping up. Then, since being mean wasn't working, I tried being nice. One time he came over and I let him in. We sat down and talked. I asked "Why do you continue to come to my house, though I have asked you not to?" His response was "Indiana, you never told me to stop coming, you always asked why I kept popping up." I thought about it and you know what, he was right. I looked him in the eye, apologized for hurting him, asked him to stop coming to my house, and suggested he move on with his life. I never saw him again.

I realized that day that though I said I didn't want him popping up, when I got lonely I thought about him, and suddenly he would pop up. It wasn't until I decided it wasn't worth it, and spoke directly to the situation, that the soul tie was broken. There will come a time when you will have to look him in the face and say, "No More!" You must decide to trust God or rely on your own strength. Face it head on and proclaim "God, I love you more."

# Chapter 4
## Christian Dating:
### Set the Standard and Stick to It

*But above all, my brethren, do not swear, either by heaven or by earth or with any other oath. But let your "Yes" be "Yes," and your "No," "No," lest you fall into judgement.*
*James 5:12 (NKJV)*

Oh how I wish we could go back to the bible days. Those days when God told the men exactly who their wife was and what she would be doing when it was time for them to meet. Things would be so much easier. Not saying that God cannot or does not do that now, but courting is certainly much different now. However I do not believe it is as hard as it seems. In my opinion dating is hard because we put the cart before the horse so to speak. Good intentions are corroded by poor expectations. What do you expect to get out of dating? If you are dating to have fun, or meet new people for example, then do just that. And if you are dating to get to know someone in hopes of finding your future spouse, then do just that as well. Whatever your intentions, the other person should be made aware.

## Rule #1 Absolutely positively NO SEX!

*Know ye not that the unrighteous shall not inherit the kingdom of God? Be not deceived: neither fornicators, nor idolaters, nor adulterers, nor effeminate, nor abusers of themselves with mankind, nor thieves, nor covetous, nor drunkards, nor revilers, nor extortioners, shall inherit the kingdom of God. - 1 Corinthians 6: 9 - 10 (KJV)*

Your body is the temple of the Holy Spirit. Don't defile your temple by letting one not sent by God intrude. Sex has become devalued and overrated in today's society. It means something to God and it should mean something to His children. You won't die or burst from not doing it, so stop believing all the lies. The more you engage in pre-marital sex the more soul-ties have to be broken before God can send you the right person. Sex is the means in which two people become one in holy matrimony. Just because yall ain't married doesn't mean you have not become one in the Spirit. That's why you can't get him off your mind. That's why you still remember when it happened and how it felt. That's why you get weak whenever you think about him or he comes around. The bible says "Be ye holy for I am holy!" Just because everybody's doing it does not make it right. He may be fine, but is he fine enough to go to hell for?

Regardless of your intention in dating, sex complicates things. Sex allows feelings to get involved, regardless of whether the person says they are or not. Allowing or giving someone your body, before they make a commitment to you, devalues your most prized possession. Regardless of what the world says, sex is never just sex!

Sex turns the attention from getting to know the other person, to self and fleshly gratification. Notice how once sex is introduced into the relationship, talks about the future, likes, dislikes, goals, dreams, etc. suddenly cease. Sex is not love. Having sex will not make him stay or make him like you more. While sex is important in a marriage, I have never heard a couple married for 10, 20, 30, or 50 years say they stayed together because the sex was good. Sex should be an act of love, not a pass time activity.

Think about it, would you want to marry someone who can have sex with no strings attached? And if so, do you believe they can be faithful?

**Rule #2 Don't be unequally yoked!**
*Be ye not unequally yoked together with unbelievers: for what fellowship hath righteousness with unrighteousness? And what communion hath light with darkness? - 2 Corinthians 6:14 (KJV)*

Going to church doesn't make you a Christian, no more than standing in the garage makes you a Cadillac! Explore his relationship with the Lord. Is he living a holy Christ-like life? Don't hook up with someone playing Christian. Being a Christian is the in thing, these days. Many claim to be a Christian, yet they do whatever they want and live however they want. The word says "if you love me, you will keep my commandments." God's word does not need defending, it is what it is. Stand on the word, and if he will not or tries to make you conform, please walk away. Don't date someone who tells you "it don't take all that." Or my personal favorite "God knows my heart." No, we are not all perfect, and yes we will make mistakes. But we cannot continue to make the same mistakes over and over and expect the blessings of God in return.

Remember there is no compromising on the word. Beware of those who twist the word in THEIR favor. If it don't agree with your teachings, WALK AWAY. Even if you don't know a particular scripture he may be attempting to quote, the Holy Ghost will give you a check in your Spirit to let you know it ain't right. Don't ignore it. WALK AWAY. You should not have to debate your beliefs or prove why you do or don't do something. WALK AWAY. Even if he is a proclaimed "Leader" in the church, WALK AWAY.

One of the many questions, many Christians have is "does he have to be a Christian?" If by Christian you mean, going to church, then my opinion is No. But I do believe that you both should believe in the same God. There are many reasons people do not attend church regularly, such as work, or past hurts or it's just never been a part of their lifestyle. But that does not mean that they have turned their back on God. We cannot beat people over the head with the bible, but we can show the love of Christ in how we live. Remember what it took and how long it took for you to finally go to church regularly. The same grace and acceptance that was extended to you should be extended to him.

**Rule #3 If you don't stand for something you will fall for anything.**
*He that hath no rule over his own spirit is like a city that is broken down, and without walls. - Proverbs 25:28 (KJV)*

Know your boundaries and standards before you start dating and why, someone can easily come along and try to change them, but if you stick to them, you will be happier. Don't compromise. Men will either live up to your standards or walk away. Don't cry/mourn over those who walk away. Especially know your sexual triggers. There is always a point of no return. If you know that if you cuddle up with him on the couch watching TV and he gets to rubbing or y'all start kissing and before you know it you in the bathroom crying and repenting, "Don't do it!" If you put the flesh in a familiar situation it will do and react familiarly. The bible says flee sexual immorality, not stand there and reason with it!

Also respect the boundaries and standards of your mate. Just because you love to kiss and it does not leave you all hot and bothered does not mean it is not a trigger for the other person. Respect is two-way, if you want respect, give respect. We are all at different stages in this Christian walk. What may be a temptation to one may not be a temptation to another. Remember the goal is to enjoy getting to know each other while maintaining a holy lifestyle that is pleasing to the Lord.

Be ready to be tested, especially when it comes to sex. If the other person is not on the same level. They will stick around for two reasons. First, to see if they can tempt you otherwise. Or two, to see if you really mean what you say. In the first scenario, they will try different things to see if you will give in. After you pass the temptation test, they will stick around as long as possible until they can no longer hold out. Most men can last about 3 months without getting any, after that they will generally walk away, unless of course they are celibate as well.

**Rule #4 Stop trying to turn Mr. Wrong into Mr. Right**
*Beware of false prophets, which come to you in sheep's clothing, but inwardly they are ravening wolves. - Matthew 7:15 (KJV)*
*Wherefore by their fruits ye shall know them. - Matthew 7:20 (KJV)*

Now days, the world looks at being single as a curse. Women would rather have "any" man than to be alone. But by doing so you are not only setting up yourself for heartache, but also creating more soul-ties, and preventing Mr. Right from coming into your life. Don't be afraid to walk away from someone, if they are not what you want. Relationships take time. The right one will come along. The sooner you walk away the easier it will be to move on. Remember there are no regrets, in standing on your beliefs. To thine own self be true!

Steve Harvey, said it beautifully, and I am paraphrasing "Stop worrying about if he likes you, but rather focus on if you like him." I would rather walk away in the first two months than to waste two years. You can't get your time back. One of the biggest regrets of failed relationships is wasted time. On the contrary, invested time is one of the reasons people stay. Allow the Holy Spirit to give you keen discernment and trust Him. As I learn and love myself more, I am most proud to walk away sooner than later from someone or something that is not good for me.

**Rule #5 Keep your eyes wide open!**
*He that walketh with wise men shall be wise: but a companion of fools shall be destroyed. - Proverbs 13:20 (KJV)*

The presence of a new beau can be exciting and your judgment can be clouded in the excitement. Pray and ask God for guidance. Talk to your friends and loved ones, they may be able to see what you can't. Dating should be fun, but remember everything should be decent and in order. Hint: If you are afraid to tell someone about him, what are you hiding? He may not be the one and you are just too scared to admit it.

I never understood how a woman can love and trust her girlfriends or BFF dearly until there is a man involved. When Mister comes into the picture, all of a sudden the girls don't understand, are jealous, single and bitter, or just "hating." Love is not blind. It is just that as women, the nurturer in us, wants to compromise too much for the presumption of love. Too many times we question what love is and forget to discuss what it is not. You cannot give up the pure essence of who you are, what you believe in, and your dreams for him. Women become blinded by the wining and dining, gifts, quality time, etc, compromise on the wrong things, and fall in love with the perceived potential of him rather than who he is.

Remember, in the beginning of the relationship, everyone brings out their best. When the fog begins to clear and the real him begins to show, stop holding on to the beginning of the romance. If he stops taking you out, stops communicating, and starts breaking promises, then understand he is showing you the real him. Believe it, and if it is not what you want, please walk away.

**Rule #6 Get out the house, make him date you!**

Date outside the home. Do not spend time, especially in the beginning, in and out of each other's homes. Make him work for it, make him date you. You are worth it. Just because you are a homebody doesn't mean you should spend time at home. The relationship should progress. If he can come to your house, lay all over your couch, kick his feet up, watch TV, bring his boys over to watch the game, and eat up your good cooking. Why would he want to marry you? Don't give all of you away too soon.

Dating is a time to get to know him. Observation of interaction with others, not just you, is the best teacher. At some point talking will become cheap and redundant. The more things you do together the better the conversation should get. There is no imagination or creativity in staying in the house. You can only watch TV, eat dinner, or have sex. Sure many will argue that you can play games, talk, read the bible, etc. and that none of that can lead to sex but let's be real. Two adults, alone, in an empty house, with no children, and no friends, to hold them accountable or keep them busy, will generally end up having sex or darn close to it.

If you play with fire you will get burned. If you think you are strong enough to cuddle on the couch and watch a movie without it leading to sex, then play on. Of course it can happen. The devil is very patient, he will let you think you are strong the first time or even the first couple of times. If you continuously put the flesh in a familiar situation it will react familiarly. You can go from zero to sixty real quick. You're on the couch, the lights go out and the movie starts. Then he asks, "Why are you sitting way over there?" "Come closer, I won't bite!" Then you are leaned up against him, legs across the couch, his arms around you, and he begins rubbing your shoulders. Next thing you know, he is whispering in your ear "are you comfortable?" Before you know it he is nibbling on your ear and rubbing more than your shoulder! Hmm...what movie were you watching?

**Rule #7 Make him respect you, especially your body.**

My pastor always says "He ain't blind, and you ain't braille." Don't allow him to touch you inappropriately. Affection can turn for the worst quickly. Holding hands and hugging are one thing. But when it leads to touching and rubbing of body parts, that's an issue. Kissing can even become inappropriate. A peck on the cheek or a peck on the lips, can turn to French kissing and yall ain't never been to France! Your body is your temple, if you allow him to roam and search, or try before he buys, what is the benefit of purchasing. Even if he says you are his woman or girlfriend, you are not his possession.

If you want a gentleman (opening doors, pulling our chairs, etc.) make him be a gentleman. Don't touch a door knob in his presence. Don't go through a door unless he opens it. Stand until he pulls out your seat. My grandmother used to tell us that a gentleman comes to the door and knocks. If he pulled up and blew the horn, she would break our necks if we even looked at the door. Now a days, technology has ruined dating. He will text "I'm outside" and we come running out the door. The automatic door unlock button, means he doesn't have to come to your side and unlock the door to let you in. But like Steve Harvey, says "Don't be the chirp, chirp girl." In other words, don't open your own door, no matter what.

Like I said before, you are worth it. Either he will step up or step away. Either way you win. Men like the thrill of the chase, they like a challenge. If it is easy for them to get you, then it will be easy for the next one to take you away. If you have and show respect for yourself, you teach others how to respect you.

## Rule #8 Don't move too fast before the relationship is defined

The world has abused the term friends. Yes you should be friends with your mate, but intimacy should not be introduced until both have determined a relationship exists. Friends don't have sex. Friends don't kiss! If the relationship is not defined, continue to treat him as your friend. Don't wait till after you kiss or have had sex to ask "where is this going?" Don't assume you are his woman, because he kissed you, you have had sex, or because you spend so much time together. Until he says it, you keep treating him like a friend, and not friends with benefits. That means kiss on the hand and the good ole church hug!

*Do not give what is holy to the dogs, nor cast your pearls before swine, lest they trample them under their feet, and turn and tear you in pieces. - Matthew 7:6 (NKJV)*

Many of women have been disappointed because they allowed or gave too much without knowing if he shared her feelings, her desire for monogamy, or her desire for a relationship. If a man says, "I'm not looking for anything serious," please believe him and don't assume you are the "good" woman that can change his mind. This is about more than just sex, this is about your heart. We must guard our hearts from hurt.

Women don't give men enough credit. They are not scared creatures, who do not know or are afraid to ask for what they want. If he can open his mouth and ask for sex, or ask whether he can come over then certainly he can ask you to be his woman. If the only time he expresses his love for you is when you are in bed having a climatic experience, you are not the one!

Sex does not imply relationship and shacking or cohabitating does not imply marriage. As Christians we not only represent ourselves and our womanhood, we represent Christ. We cannot continue to do as the world does yet expect a different result. Because we are Christ in the Earth, we may be the only God he sees. If you are like the other chicks he has dated, why would he want to make you his wife. As Christians there is no new standard of dating to create, the standard is already set, it's called the Bible. There is no compromising with the word of God, regardless of how good it feels, or whether everybody is doing it.

### Rule #9 Don't be afraid to be you. Keep it 100.

*In God I have put my trust, I will not be afraid. What can man do to me? - Psalm 56:11 (NKJV)*

Dating is a time to get to know the other person. The best thing you can do is stay true to yourself. In the beginning of a relationship, we try to impress each other. However, when the dust or newness settles, the real person comes out. Stop worrying about whether he likes you. Remember ladies, you hold the cards. Be more concerned about whether you like him!

Unfortunately this does not just apply to women. If he does not like what he sees or hears, he can move on just like you.

Pray for discernment and when God shows you the real person, don't be afraid to walk away. As women we are nurturers, and this can be a bad thing. We always want to give a person the benefit of the doubt and are hopeful that they will change. We hold on to the good times, or we convince ourselves that he has the potential to be what we want him to be. News Flash: It is God's job to change people NOT yours! If he is not what you want in the beginning, don't assume he will be that later. The sooner you walk away, the lesser the heartache. Back in the day, my relationships were all long term, I mean, I was with my high school sweetheart for 8 years. The next guy for 2 years, then 4 years, then 2 years again and so forth. But they were all wrong for me. Yet I stayed, hoping we would get back to the good ole days. Now I find joy in walking away from someone I just met and his conversation was wrong, or he did or didn't do the right thing. I refuse to give someone 2, 3, 4 plus years and we are on different levels. I thank God for discernment and the ability to stand on His word.

Voice your opinion. If you don't like something or something feels wrong, don't be afraid to speak up. Men can't read your mind. Speak your mind and you will be happier. You will eliminate the "pressure pot" scenario: allowing things to build up until you can't take it anymore, then the lid pops off! The worst thing that can happen is you break up or he doesn't call you. Either way, you win. On to the next one.

Know what you want and don't be afraid to voice it. If you want to be married, say it. If you are just having fun, say it. Either way, own it and if he is not on the same level, walk away. Know who you are, and don't be afraid to show it. I love God, if a guy says "it don't take all that" or calls me "pseudo-saint", I walk away. Personally, I don't think I am a pseudo-saint but if a guy thinks enough to point that out, then his lifestyle definitely is not conducive to the Christian life style I stand for. Remember, if someone doesn't like what you are doing or what you are about, and if you can't give that thing up, then walk away. Doing so will save you a lot of arguments in the long run.

Dating is also about compatibility. Can the two of you come together and go forward together in peace and happiness? No you will not agree on everything. But every value and standard is not up for negotiation. Determine what your deal breakers are and stick to it. Sometimes, you may not know what your deal breakers are, until you are confronted with it. When you realize it, own it, voice it, and yes, Walk Away!

**Rule #10 Dress to Impress**

If you don't want him to treat you like a W****, stop dressing like one! If he can see everything you've got, why would he want to explore deeper? The energy you put out is the energy you receive. You might be constantly getting approached by "dogs" because you're acting like you're in heat. When did "Naked" become the new "Sexy?" If you want him to be attracted to your mind, stop leading with your body!

There is a thin line between classy and trashy. No man wants to take trashy to meet his mother or to a business dinner or event. Men are visual and yes they want their woman to be sexy. But all attention is not good attention. Breasts hanging out in that low cut blouse, butt hanging out in them low-rider jeans, or dress or pants so tight that he knows what you ate for dinner or what is in your pocket are not the attire of a wife. Conservative does not mean boring. But trashy does mean on the hunt, it implies you are not taken and are looking for attention.

Remember, as Christians we are not to be indulging in sexual activity. If your clothing is inappropriate, how can you expect him not to want sex or to keep his hands to himself? What crosses your mind as you are getting ready for your date? How you dress implies your expectations. Did you pick out that matching panty and bra set? Did you reach for that sexy dress that hugs all your curves the right way? Don't be alarmed if he can't look you in your eyes.

Yes your style of dress should match your personality. However it should not be a direct conflict with your values, standards, and desires for a mate. If you want a husband, dress like a wife not the side chick!

# Chapter 5
## Dealing with Loneliness:
## If You Don't Like You, He Won't Either

*Let your conduct be without covetousness; be content with such things as you have. For He Himself has said, "I will never leave you nor forsake you."*
*Hebrews 13:5 (NKJV)*

The discussion of and even the mere mention of "loneliness" is profanity to singles. How dare one insinuate that one is lonely simply based on the lack of being in a relationship? A relationship will not and does not eliminate loneliness. So what makes others assume that you are lonely?

First, loneliness is assumed because you said it. Maybe you didn't use those exact words, but remember actions speak louder than words. All you talk about is relationships. If you had a man. Why men fail to commit. Why men cheat. Why women take advantage of good men. Why men are afraid of marriage. Why it seems like bad girls or sinners always have a man. Why men are afraid of being in a relationship without sex. How to attract Mr. Right. What to do or not do when dating. When you get a man, how you would and would not treat him. When you get a man, what you would do or begin doing. Blah, blah, blah. Yet all your theories have not been tested because it has been so long since you had a relationship or you are afraid to get into a relationship due to fear of failure. People around you are so tired of hearing and discussing relationships, that they just come out and ask you "Are you lonely?"

Secondly, loneliness is assumed because your life is void of activities and you isolate yourself. I'm bored. There is nothing to do in this town. I don't have anyone to hang out with. You have established a routine of work, home, and church. And when you are challenged to step outside of your comfort zone, you make excuses. I don't have money for that. I can't do that alone. A Christian should not be found in that place or doing that. I don't have time for that. Ironically you have plenty of time to complain and throw a pity party.

Loneliness is also assumed because you make poor choices in men. He's not that bad. He has potential. Two out of three ain't bad. No person is perfect, we have to make compromises. Perhaps this is true, but your character, your integrity, or your salvation should not be compromised. Loneliness can make a person sacrifice all their desires and morals for the temporary relief of being with someone.

Loneliness is also assumed because you refuse to allow the void to be filled in other ways. I'm tired of being around women all the time. Perhaps your girlfriends can not take the place of a man. But truth is, you don't have a man and being miserable is not going to attract him to you. Girlfriends and other activities are not meant to take the place of a man they are meant to bring fulfillment and help you discover who you are and what you want.

Loneliness is assumed because you have put your life on hold. You have put your dreams in a box and set them aside, waiting for that man to come along and help you dust the box off and inspire you to attempt them. Yes we all want support and encouragement. But what if, Mr. Right is on the journey to fulfilling those dreams that you have placed in that box. If you never attempt to go after them, then you may never meet Mr. Right.

All your needs, all your activities, all your conversations, all of your actions or lack thereof should not be tied to a man or relationship. Doing so will make you miss out on life. God does not give us a spouse to complete us. He brings together two complete persons to do the work of the kingdom. The two of you together should be able to do more for the kingdom, than you are able to do alone.

Singles should not be ashamed of being lonely. It is normal and is a very human emotion. Loneliness, however, is "the constant state of being lonely." This constant state can lead to issues. At the end of the day, when girlfriends go home, when the party is over, when something great happens and you have no one to share it with or when you place the key in the door and no one is there to greet you. How do you handle the silence? How do you handle the pain? When no one is looking, what do you do? Cry yourself to sleep, turn to comfort foods, call Mr. Right Now? It is this person, the person that you don't want anyone to know about that God wants to commune with.

*But I want you to be without care. He who is unmarried cares for the things of the Lord – how he may please the Lord. But he who is married cares about the things of the world – how he may please his wife. And this I say for your own profit, not that I may put a leash on you, but for what is proper, and that you may serve the lord without distraction. – 1 Corinthians 7: 32, 33 & 35 (NKJV)*

Loneliness is a distraction. Too much time in this state distracts you from the place that God wants you to be, the life He wants you to live, and yes the person He has for you. God wants us to be content and happy, in whatever state we are in. Loneliness and the things it makes us do are not signs of happiness. Until you learn to deal with the loneliness, to acknowledge the feeling, and move on quickly, you will not be ready for Mr. Right.

Too much time in this state is a sign that the flesh is in control. Spirit and flesh are battling and flesh is winning. Again until you learn to deal with the flesh, stop calling Mr. Right Now, you will continue to go through the same test. Yes Mr. Right Now is a test and every time you call him, you fail the test. Many think Mr. Right Now is the same person, but he can be a different person but yield the same results. We all know the scripture, "be angry and sin not," well as singles we must learn to be lonely and sin not as well. Every time you satisfy your fleshly desires, you fail the test. As I said before, we must get to the "God, I love you more" mentality to finally pass the test. In a sinful world, that implores one to do whatever makes them happy, it is difficult but not impossible.

So how do we deal with the loneliness? Great girlfriends and activities are a great start. But to fight loneliness we have to fight in the Spirit. I love Joyce Myers, she is my favorite author and speaker. She has a series on You Tube entitled "Dealing with Loneliness." In it, she gave some great tips on dealing with loneliness.

First, Joyce Myers gave an interesting definition of loneliness: to feel that you are deserted. I had never thought of it this way. I always viewed loneliness as the longing for a significant other. Mrs. Myers pointed out that loneliness is caused by our desire to be understood and accepted. When things happen in our lives, good or bad, not everyone will be happy or sympathize. We must look to God. We must learn to please God and follow our hearts.

In order to not be lonely we must know that God is always with us. We all know the scripture "God will never leave nor forsake us." But do we really believe that. We must be consciously aware of that. Joyce Myers advises to say it out loud, every day, two, three, or however many times as needed, until the light bulb comes on. Rejection is part of life. Attempting to please everyone leads to confusion. To be aware that God is with us means to see what God is doing in our lives. God is always working on our behalf. Angels are assigned to us. Learn to listen to God. The more of His word you put into you, the more the Holy Spirit can recall in your time of need.

The first thing the enemy wants to do when you are in a state of distress or facing any difficulties is tell you that you are alone, no one understands you, that you are in this by yourself. That is a lie from the pit of hell. You are never alone. Sometimes things in life and loneliness hit you so hard, it literally leaves you speechless. In my times of loneliness, sometimes my thoughts are so loud and out of whack that I can't focus on reading the bible. I listen to music, gospel music, to drown out the thoughts and bring me back into God's presence. Once the thoughts subdue, then I can read the word. I have learned that crying myself to sleep isn't bad. Tears can be a sign of communication to God. He understands our tears, when we are speechless, our spirit cries out for us. The word says "weeping may endure for a night but joy comes in the morning." The next day I awake refreshed and ready to tackle any issues. Most times I awaken realizing that things weren't as bad or as important as they seemed. But most importantly, I awaken and the lonely feeling has passed. There is ministry and comfort in tears.

Secondly, Joyce Myers pointed out, to not be lonely, you must know how to be with yourself. At the end of the day, there will always be you. Learn to love yourself. Get to know yourself: what you like, what you enjoy, and what makes you happy. Be yourself. Learn to be comfortable and content with you and enjoy life. Many people use the scripture "And God said it is not good for man to be alone," as an excuse to justify not enjoying being alone. You will be unable to find someone, even when married, who will be there 24/7 for you. A spouse has to go to work, or will have activities outside of you. Friends will be busy. Loved ones will pass away. Life happens. You are the only consistent person in your life, might as well enjoy her! I have found that I really do enjoy spending time alone. I enjoy listening to music as I clean my house. I enjoy reading a good book when nothing interesting is on television. And I enjoy writing. Writing has become therapeutic as well as a great hobby. I am a homebody, and I am ok with that. I used to feel something was wrong with me because I wanted to stay home. Truth is I have always been a homebody, but people told me I was lonely so I did other stuff to fit in. Now don't get me wrong, I do get bored. Sometimes the quietness makes me want to scream, and sometimes I have to tell my own self to shut up. In those times, I turn to my girlfriends, church members, and my meetup groups.

My meetup groups have been the best discovery ever! I used to be one of those women who said, "I don't hang around a lot of women, women are messy, I have one or two friends, and that's how I like it, my circle is small and tight." That is a lie and an excuse to remain in misery. All women are not messy. If all you encounter is messy people, you may be the problem, you attract what you are. In one year my BFF got married, and I lost my job. Now my BFF didn't have time and those close co-worker relationships were gone. As my co-workers found new jobs I was alone most of the day. I had nothing to do. I forgot who suggested meetup.com but I logged on and there were groups for every activity you could think of. I found fitness groups, singles groups, entrepreneurial groups, coffee groups, movie groups, dining out groups, wine enthusiasts' groups, and religious groups. Every activity I ever wanted to do or try but had no one to go with me, there was a group for. Once I got over the fear of meeting new people, I jumped in. Each group has activities either once a week or once a month. If I feel like hanging out I go and if not I don't. The beauty is I have met great people, formed new relationships, and don't worry about not having someone to do things with. I even formed my own group for single women based on the feedback I received from my first book.

Exploring new activities has helped me to realize that though I am not as spontaneous as I like, I am more adventurous than I thought. I love trying new things. I also learned that I am a big fan of the arts: plays, music, dance, etc. I am also an advocate and supporter of my race, the African American community in film, arts, etc. I love independent movies….Go Netflix! The more you learn about yourself, the more you will have to offer when Mr. Right comes along. When asked "what do you like to do?" You will have more to say than going out to dinner, going to the movies, and hanging out with friends. Please note this is a basic answer, and implies that you really don't know what you like to do and will probably be clingy in a relationship (in my opinion).

If you don't like you, he won't either! Like spirits attract. You cannot claim to be this wonderful, exciting, and great woman of God in one breath, then in the next claim to be depressed about not having a man asking "what's wrong with me?" You must learn to accept the good and the not so good in yourself. The sooner you discover you, the sooner you will learn the good far outweighs the bad. God knows it all and LOVES you anyway!

# Chapter 6
## Examine Yourself: Like Spirits Attract

*But the Lord said to Samuel, "Do not look at his appearance or at his physical stature, because I have refused him. For the Lord does not see as man sees; for man looks at the outward appearance, but the Lord looks at the heart."*
1 Samuel 16:7 (NKJV)

It's time to put the big girl panties on and face the hard truth. As women we are very hard on ourselves. We judge ourselves harshly for mistakes. We allow others to speak negativity into our spirits, and brush it off, claiming to be "strong" or having "tough skin." We continue to keep people in our circles and allow people into our circles that we know mean us no earthly good. We nurture others, while neglecting ourselves. We consistently advocate, encourage, and support others while failing to seek the same ourselves. We are the number one cheerleaders for our men, our children, our friends, our family, and yes even our enemies. We wish the best for everyone, we expect the best of everyone, and we attempt to be the best for everyone. Yet when it comes to matters of the heart, we are bleeding internally and fail to seek help.

The world has told us that it is weak to show too much emotion or to ask for what we need. Don't wear your heart on your sleeves! It don't take all that! Don't get your panties in a bunch! You should be happy to get what you have! Your standards are too high! Even when it comes to having or finding Mr. Right we have allowed society to dictate to us what a man requires. Lose weight. Gain weight. Learn to cook, a way to a man's heart is through his stomach. Men are visual, make yourself more attractive. Be sexier. You're too independent, men like to be needed. Men are intimidated by your education and success. You're being unrealistic, lower your standards. All men cheat. Etc., Etc., Etc.

If you are waiting on God to send you your husband, why do you seek answers to your prolonged singleness from the world? Only God can answer the question as to why His gift has yet to come. Since we know that Mr. Right will come in God's perfect timing, perhaps rather than asking God "Why am I still single?" the more appropriate question is "God, what do you want me to do in my singleness to prepare for my husband." The answer is simple. As women we are quick to point out what's wrong with us, but it is what's right with us that is of concern to God. We must get in a position, to allow God to show us our heart. The "bad" in you is not keeping you from receiving Mr. Right. It is the inability to see the good in yourself that is prolonging the wait.

Revealing of one's heart is a twofold process. First God must show you your faults and secondly he must show you what he sees. While painful, the purpose is not for you to fix everything (it may be impossible) but to bring awareness so that you are more acceptable of yourself and others thus allowing God to help. The more you learn of your own imperfections the more acceptable you are of the imperfections of others. The more you see the good in yourself, the more aware you are of your worth, and able to attract that same good from others. Let's explore our hearts, shall we.

In order to explore our hearts, we must actively seek God's presence. I know this is redundant, but it must be said again. We must commit to getting in the face of God daily. No excuses. We also must commit to the process. Giving up is not an option. How bad do you want Mr. Right? Are you worth the wait? Are you worth your healing and deliverance? Do you truly want the love you seek or are you so afraid that you have convinced yourself that it doesn't exist? When God starts to reveal the inner you, it is a scary road. You will find out you are not as cute as you thought you were.

*And you have forgotten the exhortations which speaks to you as to sons: "My son, do not despise the chastening of the Lord, nor be discouraged when you are rebuked by Him; for whom the Lord loves He chastens, and scourges every son whom He receives. - Hebrews 12: 5-6 (NKJV)*

When you are tempted to run. Remember He is doing it out of love. Marriage is about two complete people coming together to become one. Remember you want love that you have never seen, love that is everlasting, true happily ever after (not to be confused with perfection or devoid of trouble or hard times), and love that endures and conquers all. That love only comes from God. Remember the point is so that God will be number one in your life. How do you run from God you ask? But putting down the Word, stop reading the bible, stop going to church and refusing to face the truth. God speaks through His word. When it gets tough and the tears begin to flow, the frustration begins to boil, the pity party starts to ignite, and you feel beaten and battered….running will be the first thing you want to do.

I remember when the Lord told me I wasn't ready for marriage because I was selfish, bitter, and did not love myself. I literally threw my bible across the bed and cried like a baby. I did not pick up the bible for weeks after that. I was hurt. Here I was thinking I was this "good woman" and "great Christian," educated, independent, in church and celibate and that wasn't enough. But each day, as I ran, I kept hearing the Lord say, "I Love you." I kept running, then I heard Him say, "Let me heal the hurt."

Becoming aware of your faults is the first step towards accepting God's healing. It's like walking around in pain, and not knowing what's wrong until you receive a diagnosis from the doctor. Once the diagnosis is received a treatment plan can be implemented. Otherwise you are just self-medicating, treating symptoms, rather than curing the illness.

Hurt people really do hurt people. It is human nature to preserve self and to prevent pain. I knew I was angry towards my mother. In my heart of hearts I love my mother. The Christian in me knew, that the word says to honor thy mother and father. But when I was in her presence I did not feel nor project love. Yes I was molested and yes I was angry at her for failing to protect me. I really wanted to let it go, but God showed me that though I wanted to let it go, my mind could not do so, because I had not told it what to do with those feelings. My heart was broken. My mind replayed the negative words spoken, the feelings of abandonment and rejection, and the missing love and support over and over. I longed for a better relationship with her but I could not let go of the past.

One day God and I had a really long, deep conversation. I was sitting in my living room, in my favorite chair and I said out loud, "God I'm tired, I want to let it go." But before this conversation, my mother got sick and she was taken to the hospital by ambulance. She did not call me right away, she waited until I got off work. On my way home, I got a phone call and she said "just letting you know I was in the hospital." When I arrived in her room, after seeing that she was stable, I asked why she didn't call me. Her response cut me deep. She said, "I didn't think you cared." At that moment, I realized that I was selfish and bitter as God had said. How could I allow my hurt to make my mother feel as if I didn't love her? And more importantly how did I expect her to feel differently when I talked to her any kind of way, got angry if she asked me to do anything, avoided her calls, fearing she was going to ask me for something, or said no to many of her requests when I could have said yes. That day I realized that I was not showing my mother the Christ in me that I proclaimed to have. To her I was a hypocrite. Rather than being angry because she was not who I wanted her to be, I decided to ask God to teach me how to love her for who she is and respect her position in my life.

I cried all the way home and when I got in the house, and told God "I'm tired, I got to fix this, I love my mother I just don't know how to let go of the pain." God showed me I needed to release it. I talked to my mother a little. One day I told her about the molestations and the bullying, but I could not bring myself to tell her I was mad at her. She was dealing with her own health issues, I felt like I would be pouring salt on the wound. Plus, I didn't see the purpose of hurting her just so I could feel better. God implored me to write a letter to my mother. I wrote the letter, and to my surprise, I felt a lot better. Then God showed me her point of view. My mother raised me the best she could with what she had. She had been hurt and abused by men and projected her hurt onto me. Her intentions were not to hurt me, but to keep me from following in her footsteps. She did not want me to do drugs, alcohol, or become a teenage mother; so she was strict. She did not know what to do when I was molested other than call the police, because nothing was done when it happened to her. I remember asking her why we never talked about the molestation, and she replied "you didn't say nothing, I thought you were ok, all he did was touch you." At the time I felt that was pretty harsh to say. But God said, "That is what was said to her."

Then God showed me that the things I hated in her, were the same things that I disliked in myself. It took me a minute to process that one. In my head I was nothing like my mother, or at least I tried hard not to be. My smart mouth, bad attitude, and stubbornness were just like her. We were both hurt, and hurting others in return. She self-medicated with drugs and alcohol. I hated this growing up. But I discovered I did the same thing, only my drug of choice was food! I allowed food to be my comforter and now God wants to be my comforter. When I met my father, I discovered he was a pimp and my mother was one of his "ladies". This hurt me at first, had a pity party for a few days, but then I realized that her years in the streets, drug and alcohol abuse were results of her sexual abuse of which I did not endure and for that I am grateful.

I would love to say my relationship with my mother is all peaches and cream now. It is not perfect but I have accepted that no matter how old I get I will always be her baby girl, she will always try to tell me what to do, and she will always be right. Growing up, I left home at 18 trying to get away from her and her lifestyle trying to prove my independence and that I didn't need her. In doing so I inflicted undue hurt and harm that no mother should have to endure from a child. Rather than choosing to be angry, I now choose to love her just the way she is. God showed me that in order to break the curse, of poverty and sexual abuse, I have to choose to allow Him to show me how to thrive as well as appreciate my mother for teaching me how to survive.

Part of allowing God to show you your faults is allowing him to show you how to change your behavior and how to mend the relationships that were hurt along the way. In addition to mending current relationships, the intention of showing you your faults is to prevent damage to future relationships. What hurt did past relationships inflict, that you are making the next man pay for?

What doesn't kill you makes you stronger and there is a lesson in every mistake are my favorite phrases. Many cite these to indicate their personal growth through triumphs. But here is another one, "if you keep going through bad relationship after bad relationship, at some point you have to begin to look in the mirror and realize you may be the problem." Every relationship, whether good or bad, gave you something you thought you needed or was missing, otherwise you would not have gotten involved in it. In chapter 3, "Breaking Soul Ties" we talked about identifying the root of our issues that caused us to make poor choices in relationships. This time I want to explore those "deal breakers" we have developed in an attempt to prevent getting hurt again. You know those things that you said will never happen again, "fool me once, shame on you, fool me twice, shame on me." We all have them, but are they realistic, and more importantly, are they Godly standards?

On the surface they appear to be great. For example at the top of my list is finding a man of integrity. He must be a man of his word. If he says he will do something, I expect him to do it. If he doesn't do it, I will write him off quickly. The problem is the men don't even know they are being tested. One day God and I were having a conversation:

God: *"You're expecting the impossible"*
Me: *"Really, God? Is it unreasonable to require honesty and communication?"*
God: *"They are not him."*
Me: *"Him who?"*
God: *"Your father. He hurt you, you are remembering his broken promises, lack of communication, and the pain and abandonment you felt as a child. Now you hold men accountable to be the father you never had. It is an impossible task because men are humanly flawed. They make mistakes. They cannot read your mind. They can be selfish at times, not taking into consideration the feelings of others. Only I can be your father. Only I can be truly honest. My word, my promises, are always valid. You must stop looking for a replacement. I have always been your father. Trust me with your heart. Trust that I will never hurt you. Trust that I will not allow you to be hurt, therefore he who I have for you will love you as I love you. Love does not eliminate the hurt, but it does eliminate malicious intent."*

Sometimes our expectations of men are impossible in that we do not account for the possibility of mistakes. Nor do we expect the ability to change. Once a cheater is not always a cheater. Once a liar is not always a liar. Once an alcoholic, drug abuser, womanizer, abuser, etc. is not always. We cannot believe in God: the God of second chances, the granter of grace and mercy, and the forgiver of our sins yet not believe that God is the same to and for all of us. Once God enters our lives, with His help we can make a 180-degree change.

What past hurts are you making the next man pay for? Sometimes they are hard to spot because they have been embedded in us so long. My issues with my father, caused me to have a lot of trust issues with men and people in general. We cannot expect our future husbands to love us past our hurts. I know it sounds good in the movies. But in reality we have to allow God to heal the hurt. Like I said, the point of examining yourself is not to give you a list of things to "fix" before you can get married. The point is awareness. It is only through awareness that one can begin the true work towards completeness.

The second part of the examination process is the opening of your spiritual eyes that you may see what God sees in you. I often hear people say "God knows my heart." But do you really know your heart? Why is this important? The heart reveals what one truly need based on who they are. Right now many women can spout out what they want in a husband quick. Many times, one can tell their maturity in Christ and their readiness for marriage, based on their answers. If a woman's want list is filled with the physical: tall, dark, handsome, 6-figure income, nice car, nice home, etc., then this woman has not tapped into what she needs. Yes we all have preferences, and physical attraction, finances, etc. are important but they will not sustain a marriage.

If we take the time to get into God's presence and ask God to show us our heart and reveal to us what we really need in a man. We will soon realize that what we thought was a priority really only scratches the surface. This is evident with the multiple relationships we have had that led to nothing. He was handsome, had a good job, nice car, and his own place yet it still didn't work out.

*The heart is deceitful above all things, and desperately wicked; who can know it? I the Lord, search the heart, I test the mind, even to give every man according to his ways, according to the fruit of his doings. - Jeremiah 17: 9-10 (NKJV)*

Until we allow the Lord to show and test our hearts, to bring out its impurities, and reintroduce us to its initial state we will continue to allow the deception and corruption from past hurts and failures to guide our lives and impact our happiness.

How do we discover the pure intentions of our heart? One way is through the eyes and words of others. Not those that despise us (although there is a bit of truth in the hate), but those who love us. God loves us unconditionally regardless. But human love develops in stages. First it is conditional, then it develops into unconditional. What do people say about you, in your presence and when you are not around? Those who have known you a long period of time, and have seen you grow and change over the years could have some valuable insight to help you discover who you are. I know it may be difficult, but you may have to ask the question: "What do you like about me?" This exercise may help you build your self-esteem, especially if you have been hard on yourself for not having someone special in your life. Many people don't like to admit they have low self-esteem, some feel it is a sign of weakness. But admittance is the first step to healing. However the answer may surprise you and help you begin the journey towards seeing your inner beauty.

While in graduate school, during a counseling class, the professor facilitated an exercise in which each person had to say what they liked about each person in the group. During that time, the person could not say anything and just had to listen. I was extremely nervous, these people had only known me a few weeks or months, and would I be able to take what they say to heart? I listened to classmates tell me they liked my intelligence and persistence, but the one that stood out the most was courageous. They felt I was courageous for sharing my stories of molestation and abuse to a room full of strangers. They told me how it helped them with their own issues and helped them to be more open themselves. Until that day I had never thought of myself as having courage. With all the things that happened to me in my past, I often was angry with myself for never speaking up for myself and thought of myself as a coward. But now I hear strangers call me courageous! That day touched me dearly. I recorded that session and still pull it out and listen to it when I get discouraged. I remember that my transparency gives others the strength to be more open.

I have another friend who always describes me as "someone who hates mediocrity." But this same friend also told me that I needed to take time to celebrate my successes more. I am always so busy setting goals for myself that once one is accomplished I move on to the next one. Rarely do I take time or even acknowledge an accomplishment. Generally no matter what I accomplish, I know that there is more to do. I have learned that this is not healthy. Every accomplishment, no matter how big or small, is worthy of celebration. Taking the time celebrate is not bragging, it is a symbol of gratefulness. My hatred for mediocrity fuels my passion to empower others to fulfil their dreams.

Poll your friends and loved ones and take inventory of the strengths they see in you. If you don't want to ask the question, pay attention to the compliments on your character. Write down what you learn.

Another way to discover the pureness of your heart is to pay attention to what you put out. People really do live by the golden rule: "Do unto others as you would have them do unto you." How many times do we hear people expressing frustration and anguish regarding how people don't treat them the way they treat others?

*Do not be deceived, God is not mocked; for whatever a man sows, that he will also reap. And let us not grow weary while doing good, for in due season we shall reap if we do not lose heart. Therefore, as we have opportunity, let us do good to all, especially to those who are of the household of faith. - Galatians 6: 7, 9-10 (NKJV)*

Yes it is better to give than to receive, but oh how we wish others would return the favor. The problem is we expect the same people we are nice to, to be nice to us. God promises we will reap, but he never said it would be from the same ones we sowed to. Ponder on this, "That in which we need, we give to others in hopes that it will be returned to us." We give time to others in hopes that time will be given to us. We give gifts to others in hopes that gifts will be given to us. We give respect to others in hopes that respect will be given to us. I could go on and on. Though we have been hurt many times by the failure to receive what we give, we still give it, with the expectation that one day someone will recognize the gift and return the gratitude.

Once you begin to pay attention to what you give, you will discover what you value. Your need is found in what you value. Then you can begin to seek relationships with men who value what you value. Why is this concept so hard in relationships? Businesses grasp it. We even grasp it when choosing our friends. But when it comes to our spouse, we seem to drop the ball. As women we stay away from messy women, who we have deemed to be not like us. But yet claim "opposites attract" when it comes to men. Businesses build partnerships and mergers based on core values.

One day in a meeting at work we were asked to put a list of core values in order of importance. Then we were asked to explain our top five. While most gave compensation as their number one value, mine was creativity. I must have the ability to use my own ideas. Your values are what is important to you and guide your actions. Clarifying your work values increases job satisfaction. So wouldn't clarifying your values also increase your relationship satisfaction? Most women proclaim to be good women, myself included. But here is a little secret….All women are good women! However not all women are good women to all men. You have to discover what makes you good, so that you know who you will be a great help mate to and vice versa.

One of the major things I give out is support and encouragement. Especially when it comes to people achieving their goals and dreams. I am quite pushy and persistent when it comes to it, too. I guess that's where the "hating mediocrity" part of me comes in at. When I think about it, support and encouragement is what I need as well. I have big dreams and I often seek the pat on the back, you can do it, or I got your back from others. I know the word says we need to encourage ourselves. But I am looking for supportiveness and motivation in my mate as well.

The point of the values exercise is to bring those things which we deem important back to the forefront. Sometimes we can get so used to not having something, or not getting something, that we believe we don't deserve it or diminish its importance. Then we begin to adapt to what we think someone else needs but end up feeling lost in the process. Your uniqueness is what will draw Mr. Right to you. The purpose of examining your heart is so that you discover your true authentic self, embrace her, and love her unconditionally. Beauty is in the eye of the beholder. It starts with you. We cannot expect Mr. Right to see and experience our beauty when we can't see it and enjoy it ourselves. Also the eyes truly are the windows to the soul. What do you see when you look in the mirror? What you see affects your perception of how others see you. If you continue to dwell on negativity, what's not right, or what could be better, you have yet to discover your true identity in Christ. God does not make mistakes. Allow him to show you your heart, so that you may begin to experience the beauty of his creation…YOU.

# Chapter 7
## Why Do You Want To Be Married?

*All the ways of a man are pure in his own eyes, but the Lord weighs the spirits (the thoughts and intents of the heart).*
*Proverbs 16:2 (AMP)*

-I want to spend the rest of my life with the man God made especially for me. I want to be married not just for love but also because it is right and my Father said sex is for marriage. I desire to grow old with my husband. – Nina

-I want to get married for the financial benefit and to raise kids in a good environment. I'll know when the right one has found me because he will make me want to be a better person which will in turn lead to me doing all the "work" that a successful marriage takes. –Belinda

-I am ready to have my "own" family. Plus I'm ready to have sex. –Alice

-I'd like to get married to share my life with my husband. Some say that marriage validates their life, I don't believe that's true. However, you do start to look around and see that everyone is paired up and have families to support them and the fear that when your parents die that there will be no one just for you. –Janet

-I'm tired of doing and being alone. I have been independent all my life. I have had to be the man and woman in my life, making decisions, sacrifices, etc. I feel that I am at a point in my life where my world is changing, for the better. The *vision for my life is coming into fruition, I am embarking on the journey of pursuing my purpose and I don't want to go alone. I want the joy of having a mate to share the intimate details of my life with, my dreams, my fears, and concerns. I want to be able to share those things without fear of being judged. To the world I have to have my "game face" on, show no weakness, but with my husband I can be free to be vulnerable. – Amanda*

*-It's the next logical step. It's time for me to settle down, have a family. There is nothing else out here to do. I'm not getting any younger, playing the field is for the youngsters! - Lisa*

*-I deserve to be married. I'm a good woman, God-fearing, active in church, saving myself for the right one. – Nina*

*-I'm ready to experience true, unconditional love. - Mona*

*-This world is not made for singles. Everybody and everything is catered to couples. It's either get married or shack up. I ain't shacking up, I'm not trying to go to hell. –Maria*

Does any of the above answers sound familiar? Believe it or not they are real answers to the question "why do you want to married?" I posed to singles on my website (names changed of course). Is there really a right or wrong answer to this question? I don't believe there is, but it is the motive or intent that deserves attention. Pureness of motives is also not the issue. I believe all these ladies were sincere. The answers appeared to come straight from their hearts. The problem then lies in the selfish connotation of the answers. Regardless of how good it sounds, all of the answers, imply some sort of positive gain from being married, rather than the unselfish act of giving of themselves to someone else.

There is a difference between "help" and "helpmate". One definition of help is "to ease the pain or discomfort of; relieve." Many seek marriage to ease their pains of financial struggles, loneliness, heartache, etc. A helpmate or helper on the other hand is "a person who contributes to the fulfillment of a need or furtherance of an effort or purpose." In other words marriage should be sought to help someone else, not to be helped, in fulfilling a need or purpose. Therefore once you recognize the value in what you "add" to the table versus the benefit in what you "bring" to the table, you are ready for marriage.

Sounds weird doesn't it. Let's explore further. In terms of food, every item brought to the table is fulfilling on its own. Basically if you eat or drink that one item, that you brought, you can get full. However it is the addition of the other items that provides a balanced meal and better nutritional value. Alone you are a conqueror, but together you are more than conquerors. By yourself, you are making it, but you have to do more with less. But with someone else, you both should do more with less stress.

One of the greatest pieces of advice, and most consistent, to singles from married people is that marriage is not easy, don't rush into it or take it lightly. It is not meant to be a scare tactic or an attempt to prevent singles from desiring or pursuing marriage. In actuality what they are saying is marriage is not a fairy tale. Contrary to the movies or Hollywood's lifestyles of the rich and famous, happily ever after does not exist. Love is an action verb, it is easy to fall in love, but hard work to stay there.

Marriage is not the cure for loneliness. Statistics show that married people still suffer from loneliness. You are still two separate people, sharing your lives together, but those lives are still separate. It is impossible to expect your spouse to spend 24/7 with you. There is work, business trips, outings and activities with friends, family, etc. No matter how much you think you may have in common, there will still be things that your spouse may want to do with others. People deserve their space to spend time with others without guilt from their spouse. Loneliness is an internal issue that cannot be resolved with external forces. No amount of time or attention will cure loneliness, only the love of Jesus can heal you. (Reread Chapter 5)

Marriage will not solve your financial worries. While you may inherit extra income, you also inherit extra debt. In addition expenses may also increase. A one bedroom apartment is certainly cheaper than a 2000 square foot house. A larger house equals larger utilities, maintenance, etc.

Remember finances is the biggest area for trouble in marriages and can lead to divorce for some. I do believe financial issues is due to lack of honesty and poor communication. Don't expect to get married and all of a sudden "come up" and want a bigger house, nicer car, better schools for the children, etc. without sitting down and really discussing money. People quickly forget the "for richer or poorer" portion of the marital vows. God promised to be your provider. Rely on God rather than man. Man is subjected to his environment: people get sick, jobs are lost, and companies downsize, and let's not forget the addition of children, all of which will be a strain on the wallet.

Sex is not an excuse to get married. Yes the bible says it is better to marry than to burn with desire. If you get married because of sex, you will want to get a divorce because of sex as well. Sex only satisfies your fleshly desires. It feels good for the moment, but marriage is for life. Good sex does not eliminate the strain of other issues. Eventually it will play out. Contrary to worldview, you will not burst from not having sex. Celibacy is possible and people do and have gotten married without pre-marital sex. While sex is important in marriage, I have never heard anyone say the "sex" is what kept the marriage together! I believe that if one is led by sex now (before marriage) they will be led by sex later (after marriage) and more prone to infidelity when they're receiving as much as they like. But that's a discussion for a different time.

Marriage is not a reward for good behavior. A righteous lifestyle does not make you deserving of marriage. Singleness is not a curse and marriage is not the ultimate blessing.

*To everything there is a season, a time for every purpose under heaven: - Ecclesiastes 3:1 (NKJV)*

God has ordained a time for singleness and a time for marriage. Both are a blessing in their appointed seasons. There is no greater value for one above the other. Each season has a purpose. Singleness proceeds marriage.

There is no way around it. We must first learn to enjoy and appreciate singleness before we delve into marriage. If it is difficult for you to enjoy your singleness, it is because you are not fulfilling its purpose. There is something God wants you to accomplish in this season, until it is done you won't be able to move on to the next. Complaining, doing nothing, having a pity party, crying, and pleading will not make God move ahead of time. Sure you can go out and find someone to marry. But then you will add additional troubles into an already difficult situation.

Marriage will not validate you. What are you trying to prove? Marriage does not prove you are worthy of love. You already have the greatest love living inside of you. Ah, let's let that sink in for a minute. As singles, do we really feel that marriage is the ultimate confirmation of love? Who are you trying to prove it to? All those who called you ugly or unattractive? Those who told you no man would ever want you? Those who said you had to do this and that to get a man? Are you trying to silence the haters? Or perhaps you are trying to prove it to yourself because deep down you actually believe what others have said over the years. You actually think singleness is a consequence of your behavior or lack of beauty! You want to show the haters that contrary to what they thought of you, somebody chose you, chose to love you, and chose to marry you. Marriage will not validate you, only God can.

Marriage will not fix it. Marriage will not fix your low self-esteem, your inability to see your own beauty, or your inability to recognize your worth. When you look in the mirror what do you see? Dark skin, pimples, scars, freckles, frown lines, dark circles under your eyes, stretch marks, cellulite, hair in the wrong places, too much fat here, not enough fat there, nappy hair, thin hair, overweight, underweight, big feet, fat feet, big head, etc.? None of that makes you more or less beautiful. The problem is not your haters, the problem is you. Other people don't determine your worth, you do! Until you see greatness in yourself, you can't expect someone else to see it. Marriage can't fix it. Only God can..... If you allow Him. Don't expect it to happen overnight. I pray every day "Lord, open my spiritual eyes, that I may see me the way you see me." Then I recite my daily confession EVERY day:

*I Am Beautiful*

*I Am Creative*

*I Am Talented*

*The world is waiting for me!*

*I Am Confident*

*I Am Strong*

*I Am Healthy*

*Each day I am closer to my goal weight.*

*This is my year. God has turned things around in my favor.*

*All things are working for my good.*

*I Am Blessed*

*My home is blessed, my businesses are blessed,*

*My finances are blessed, my relationships are blessed,*

*I am a blessing to others.*

*I am the head and not the tail. I am above and not beneath.*

*I am the lender and not the borrower.*

*I am Purpose. I am the righteousness of Christ*

*Thy Will be done in me!*

*In Jesus Name, AMEN!*

Positive confession produces positive results. If you say it every day, soon you will begin to believe it. The lie the devil told is still a lie. We make it true when we believe it and allow it to dictate our actions. It's time to stop accepting and allowing the negativity of others to hold us back. Marriage cannot fix you. Everything God made is good and perfect. Hold your head up and walk in victory.

Marriage will not complete you. Jerry McGuire messed women up. Yes a spouse should bring out the best in you. But God did not create half persons. Marriage is only as good as your singleness. Until you learn to be separate, unique, and whole, ALL BY YOURSELF, you are not yet ready for marriage. Many look to marriage to improve them or their present circumstances. Yes two are better than one and the two of you should be better and do more together than apart. But marriage does not improve your singleness, it exposes it (Myles Munroe). Right now all your defects are hidden, no one knows but you and God. But once you are married, you invite someone else into your intimate quarters. I hear many women, I'm guilty myself, say how they will change this and that about themselves when they get married. We say we will cook more, clean more, be the best communicators, never deny sex, etc., etc., blah, blah, blah! Who you are now, is who you will be when you get married. If you don't like to cook now, you will not cook more then. If you don't like cleaning now, you will not like cleaning then. Maybe you will be able to put up the façade for a few months, but trust me eventually the real you will surface. We have to stop looking at marriage as this fairy tale event that will catapult us into the best person ever. You should be the best person ever now. It is those best qualities that attract others to you. If you are waiting till marriage to let it all out, then you will keep attracting the wrong person.

God said it was not good for man to be alone (isolated, secluded, exclusive, solitary, all in one). He never said it was not good for man to be single. You don't need a spouse to fulfill your purpose. But you do need other people. A spouse is not the answer to all your issues, YOU are! You are so busy looking for someone else, you don't have time to be your true, unique, genuine self. Until you can truly embrace your singleness, you are not ready for marriage. God created male and female, not husband and wife. Singleness is more important than marriage and is the foundation of all relationships. If marriage were so important, why was Jesus single? Why did He not pursue a wife?

*But I say to the unmarried and to the widows; it is good for them to remain even as I am. – 1 Corinthians 7:8 (NKJV)*

*But I want you to be without care. He who is unmarried cares for the things of the Lord – how he may please the Lord. But he who is married cares about the things of the world – how he may please his wife.*

*And this I say for your own profit, not that I may put a leash on you, but for what is proper, and that you may serve the Lord without distraction. -1 Corinthians 7:32, 33, 35 (NKJV)*

The purpose of singleness is to serve the Lord without distraction. God designed a specific purpose for every stage in our lives. Again I say if you have not found yourself married yet, perhaps you are not fulfilling and pursuing your purpose. Your relationship with Christ is the most important aspect of your singleness. Many fear being labeled "pseudo saint", "holier than thou," or "sanctified" by others who proclaim, "It don't take all that". Actually it does take all that and some. It takes all that to remain holy and grounded in a sinful world. It takes all that to receive the promises of God. It takes all that to ensure your ticket to heaven. It takes all that to be all that God destined you to be. Faith and obedience moves God. Going with the flow, pleasure seeking or people pleasing does not move God, rather it prolongs the wait.

God does not withhold any good thing from his children. Adam did not know he needed a wife, nor did he ask God for a wife. Even though there was no one in the garden who looked like him, He was content doing what God commanded him to do. **Side note: When God said 'it is not good for man to be alone, he was reflecting on His own feelings. He created man in His own image, so that He could have someone like Him to commune with.** But now when God presented Eve to Adam....Adam was like lookie here "bone of my bone, flesh of my flesh" or in the words of Fred Flintstone "Hubba, Hubba!" When the time is right, God's appointed time, marriage will happen. There will come a time when you will look back on this time, your singleness, and think "I'm glad I wasn't married then."

The consensus among married women is that "Marriage happened when they least expected it, they were not looking, they were focused on them (their purpose and their relationship with God), and then all of a sudden he showed up." If what you are doing intensifies your desire for a mate, then you are busy doing the wrong thing. As I pointed out in my last book "Stop Asking Me Why Am I Single," we must focus on God's work not just busy work. Busy work will have you disgusted, tired, unfulfilled and unhappy. But God's work brings joy, contentment, confidence, it builds faith, and it refreshes. It is an absolute joy to know that you are constantly in His presence and in His will, which is God's definition of abundant life.

The world may say that something is wrong with you because you are not in a relationship. But remember that you are set aside by God for His glory…..ONLY if you trust Him! Trust that his plans are not your plans. Your timeline may not match his timeline. He has not forgotten you and He will grant you your desire to be married. Until then I implore you to stay in His presence. In His presence there is peace and fullness of joy. When people ask you "why are you single?" *Side note: This question is only presented to those who portray unhappiness, because the one for you, will not ask, but will be glad that you are.* But if and when they ask, reply "In God's perfect timing." Enjoy God, enjoy life, and enjoy singleness. Be the best you for you, not someone else.

Until your relationship with yourself is right, you will be unable to form a lasting, meaningful relationship with someone else. Don't allow your personal issues with being single to force you into a situation you are not prepared for. You bring to the marriage, all that you are as well as all that you are not as a single person. Stop worrying about marriage.

*Therefore do not worry about tomorrow, for tomorrow will worry about its own things. Sufficient for the day is its own trouble. - Matthew 6:34 (NKJV)*

Anytime we worry about things to come, we take away from the joy of the moment. God is with you now, He is not in the future waiting for you to get there. Singleness is not a punishment. Rather than trying to avoid it (you should know by now you can't any way), embrace it, and embrace you. The more single you become, the more worth you are to the other person – Myles Munroe. Stop worrying about the when, where, and who of marriage. Get busy being single and you will be married before you know it!

# Chapter 8
## Praying for Your Husband: The List

*Be anxious for nothing, but in everything by prayer and supplication with thanksgiving, let your requests be made known to God; and the peace of God, which surpasses all understanding, will guard your hearts and minds through Christ Jesus.*
*Philippians 4: 6-7 (NKJV)*

Many quote Philippians 4:6 but do we really abide by it? If we are truly honest, we are at anxiety to the tenth power before we actually go into prayer. Let's examine this closely:

**Be anxious for nothing** - Anxious is defined as "uneasy and apprehensive about an uncertain event or matter; worried." "Anxious" is the adjective, "nothing" is the subject and "be" is the verb. So this phrase can be rearranged as "For nothing be anxious." "For nothing be uneasy." "For nothing be uncertain." "For nothing be worried." In other words, all the anxiousness, uneasiness, uncertainty, and worry is for nothing. Then he goes on to tell us how....

***But in everything by prayer and supplication*** – Supplication is defined as "to ask for humbly or earnestly, as by praying." So if supplication is a form of prayer why did God say it twice? To intensify its meaning. Humble is the difference. There is a difference between a regular prayer and a humble prayer. Humble is defined as "marked by meekness or modesty in behavior, attitude, or spirit, not arrogant or prideful. Showing differential of submissive respect. Low in rank, quality, or station, unpretentious or lowly." In other words, stop being stubborn, humble yourself and ask for help. Jesus knows asking for help is hard for us, we like to figure things out on our own, and fix things ourselves.

***With thanksgiving*** – Thanksgiving is defined as "an act of giving thanks; an expression of gratitude, especially to God." In others words, like the Saints of old used to say, "Thank him in advance." This requires confidence in knowing that when you ask for help it will be given. Whether you see it or not, Thank Him. Regardless of what the current situation looks like, Thank Him.

***Let your requests be made known to God*** - God is urging us to develop a better communal relationship with Him. This is the third time in one verse where God is saying "just talk to me." (Prayer, supplication, let your requests be known to God) He is the only one who can help. We waste valuable time and energy internalizing issues and going to others for advice. We can't fix it and they surely can't fix it.

So Philippians 4:6 can be summed up as "Don't worry, humble yourself and ask for help. Regardless of the situation I am here, as only I can fix it. Thank Me in the midst." And if you do so

***Philippians 4:7 "And the peace of God, which surpasses all understanding, will guard your hearts and minds through Christ Jesus" (NKJV)***

Once we learn to use prayer as our first resource rather than our last resort. We not only avoid anxiety and stress but we gain the peace of God and protection of our hearts and minds. Philippians 4:6 is the command,

and Philippians 4:7 is the promise. God always provides a promise or reward for following His commands.

Many use the Philippians scripture as foundation to things they want from God or things they face in daily living like food, clothing, jobs, financial issues, etc. But this is the first time I have felt a pulling to use it when desiring a husband. The reason is, because like those same life issues, the desire for a husband has consumed and overwhelmed the thoughts of singles that God is saying to just stop. Stop worrying, stop stressing, stop wasting time and energy, He already knows that you want a husband. There is no need to allow that desire to control your life. He is in control and He is concerned about you. Relax and let him handle it. Every time the thought comes into your mind, go into prayer.

The older ladies used to tell the younger women to write down everything they wanted in a husband, put it in their bible, and watch God. I like this concept because it urges you to say (write) what you want then physically give it to God (by placing it in your bible). I'm sure we've all been told this before and may have even done it before. I remember writing my first list in my twenties, though I don't remember what was on it. A few years ago a co-worker, who has been married over 20 years urged me to write another list. This time I took a different approach, I prayed first, and asked God to reveal to me what I needed rather than what I wanted in a mate.

Your list should serve as a mirror! What, you weren't expecting that. Yes your list should be a mirror for you to examine yourself. It should let you know why you desire what you want and whether you are living according to the same standard you have set. You attract what you are. Let's look at my list:

1. He must be God-fearing. He must love the Lord and abide by his commandments. (You will know them by their fruits – Matt 7:16) Going to church every Sunday does not make a man God-fearing. I get tired of meeting men, who are active in church, even in leadership in

church, yet Monday – Saturday they act like heathens. Using their inability to control themselves, hiding behind scripture while ignoring others, to justify their ungodly behavior. Or my favorite line "God knows my heart." Sorry sir, but God knows your heart is turned away from him. We have to be careful not to let others twist the word of God for their benefit. God-fearing does not mean perfection. We all make mistakes, but don't lie on God. Hebrews calls us to be not only hearers but doers of the word. Our love for God gives us the desire and strength to keep his commandments. We cannot request the Godly union of marriage living an unrighteous lifestyle. God will not bring what is holy into an unholy place. Are you God-fearing?

2. He must love unconditionally. In 1 Corinthians 13: 1-8, we learned what love is and what it is not. Therefore we can conclude love is a decision followed by action. Marriage has waves. One minute you are up and the next you are down. The vows even state for richer or poorer, better or worse, in sickness and health. In order for you to recognize unconditional love in someone else it must first begin in you. Are you forgiving toward yourself? Do you love yourself unconditionally? Or are you highly critical of yourself? As women we often say, myself included, "I am harder on myself than I am on others." We assume this statement shows an act of more compassion towards others. But in reality it shows lack of self-love. Not stating we should not examine ourselves and seek self-improvement. But to be hard on yourself is not love. You should not beat yourself up for your mistakes. God does not condemn us, he corrects us with love and teaches us how to do better. Rather than harboring on your faults, play up your strengths. How does he treat those closest to him? His parents, children, co-workers, etc.? Do you love unconditionally?

3. Respectful of my dreams/goals and helps me achieve them. I am not stay-at-home wife material, not that I couldn't be in the future. But now, I have big dreams. Respect means that he will not laugh or spit in my face at the thought of my dreams. Respect also means that he will

deem them as important as his. Some men want their wives/girlfriends to be their biggest cheerleader and I agree with that. But women want the same. We should believe in each other's dreams and goals. I believe that God unites people in purpose. So if our dreams are going in different directions we probably will not make a good couple. Can you respect and support the dreams of your mate?

4. Sees me as his queen and most beautiful woman. Yes I know beauty is in the eye of the beholder. Yes I know I am beautiful. But so is every woman out there. I guess this requirement goes back to the unconditional love point. Beauty is based on more than physical attraction. In order to be treated as a Queen I know that he must be treated as a King.

5. Supportive and Motivational. Like I said I have big dreams. Sometimes I need to be pushed. Most times I need to be encouraged. The drive and determination required to make your dreams come true is tiring and stressful. When things go off course, as they sometimes will, your mate will need to be there to inspire you not to give up. Are you supportive and motivational?

6. Always truthful. He must be a man of integrity and honesty. He should do what he says he will do. Your word is your bond. Your gifts can take you places, but character will keep you there. I practice brutal honesty. That does not mean that I seek to hurt people, but it does mean that I aim to tell the truth regardless of whether it may hurt. My most valuable friendships are with people who are not afraid to tell me the truth. I have great respect for them. Now I do believe you should give a little sugar with your salt to sweeten the blow. You can't continue to tear people down and make no effort to build them up. That's the difference between a critical person and a truthful person. Are you always truthful?

7. Mindful of my feelings and concern for my well-being. The bible says that the husband is the head of the wife and that wives are to be

submissive to their husbands. When women are not submissive, I believe it's because they don't believe their husbands have their best interests at heart. The role of head of household, should not be taken lightly. Before marriage, we need to witness his decision making skills, ability to communicate, and our own role. Yes women, do you allow him to be the man? In my past relationships I didn't trust that anyone could take care of me but me, so I did not allow the men to be men. I did everything. Yes, I wore the pants in the relationship. That is not Godly and I had to learn to trust God first, and then others.

8. Protect and provide emotionally, physically, and financially. This one is self-explanatory but I would like to add that he has to have the drive to provide. Most men are driven by money, power, or title. I want a man driven by the desire to take care of his family. Money, power, and title can all be taken away at a blink of an eye. But a man driven by provision for his family is not prideful. He will do whatever, whenever for his family. Because of my background, growing up in poverty, I am very driven and it is the source of my independence. You would be surprised that I have met men who did not understand that. I remember an ex told me to quit my job to go after a volunteer position that I thought would propel me toward my dreams. His explanation was "God will provide." Yes sounds good, but God did not tell me to quit my job at that time. Quitting would have left me with no income, no unemployment, nothing. From that point on I no longer respected him.

9. Financially stable. Many men take this to mean they have to have a lot of money. But I mean he must have his own car, house, and career. He must have not only a dream but a vision and a plan to get there. It also means he must be taking good care of himself and his obligations. I love a man with a plan. I am a woman with a plan and also a planner. So I tend to attract men who need direction. I have no problem with that, but I don't want to take the reins and take over the head of household role.

10. No children or if he has children, being a great father with time and money. Absolutely no baby mama drama. There is nothing less attractive than a dead beat dad. I have taken a lot of flak for this one, but I am sorry, there are no exceptions to this rule. How can a man want to love and take care of me yet not take care of his own flesh and blood? I am absolutely allergic to baby mama drama. I know there are evil women out there who are spiteful and try to use the children to hurt the men. But I believe it can be fixed, with God, forgiveness, and a humble apology. I don't have kids, while I don't object to becoming an instant mom, I have a big problem with inherited stress and drama.

11. Likes to travel. There is a big beautiful world out there and I want to see it. I am not waiting to get married to start traveling. I go on a trip out of the country once a year, something I started about 6 years ago. I want to not only continue it but increase it. I have a bucket list of countries and cities I would like to visit. Comparing stamps on a passport would be a great first date! I have met men with a fear of flying or who had the inability to obtain a passport and it was a complete turn off.

12. Friendship first. He must take the time to date me and get to know me. I know that sounds redundant. But in today's world people want to jump right into a relationship and right into sex. Only to find themselves miserable 3 months later. God had to deal with me on this one. I wanted someone to take time with me but I was impatient. I would meet someone, then a month later, praying asking God if he was my husband! I had to learn that I had to be patient and allow him to date me. Time will uncover true intentions. If he only wants sex, time will tell. If he is abusive, time will tell. If he is unstable financially, time will tell. God showed me that all that I desired in a mate was only discoverable over time. Women, we cannot confuse friendship with "showing him you would make a good wife." There is such thing as doing too much. In the words of Steve Harvey, "Don't take on the role

of wife to a man who is not your husband." Spending the night at each other's home is too much. Cooking dinner every day and every weekend is too much. Washing and ironing his clothes every week is too much. Shacking is too much. Him paying all your bills is too much. If you are doing everything as his friend, or girlfriend, what incentive does he have to marry you?

13. Looking for a wife, not still playing the field. Contrary to popular belief men do know what they want and they do know when and if they are ready for marriage. I believe what a man says. It is not my job to change a man, that's what God does. I know my place. I believe that discussing marriage does not scare a man away. Now I am aware that every man I date or meet may not be "the one" and vice versa, but we should both be like minded in that we desire marriage in the future. And I'm sorry "Yes I would like to get married one day" is not a good answer. What that says to me is you're still playing the field or looking for something better.

14. Great communicator. I want someone I can be vulnerable with and talk to about anything and vice versa. Communication is the key to holding marriages and relationships together. Communication is like respect, you have to give it to get it.

15. Understands who I am past, present, and future. I am very verbal about my past, who I am now, and where I want to be in the future. While I am over my past, it still has lasting effects on who I am and what makes me tick.

My list is long in my opinion, but I have heard and seen some a lot longer. I notice that my list is filled with character attributes. Like I said your list should serve as a mirror and cause you to examine yourself as to whether you exhibit those same qualities. I believe that if they made it on your list, it is because you give out those things but fail to receive them in return. I mentioned earlier that we really do live by the golden rule of treating others the way we want to be treated. If you find that you are lacking in an area, ask the Lord to help you and show you how to do better. You cannot ask for what you are not willing to give.

Your list should also serve as a standard when dating. We should be like Santa Claus, making a list and checking it twice. If the list was made with purest desires and intentions, rather than selfish gain, when you meet someone pull out your list. But give yourself time for his true character to reveal itself. Sometimes it is not God who is slow to respond but rather our own impatience. If you check the list and you cannot answer the questions, then give it more time. If you check your list, and you begin to make excuses, then you may need to walk away.

Your list can also serve as your accountability tool. They say love is blind. New love is beyond blind, if there is such word. The newness of a relationship leaves us all giddy, naïve, and clueless. In the beginning both parties put on their absolute best. Enjoy spending time with each other, but break out that list at least once a month and do some deep examinations. Regardless of how good it is, don't allow yourself to settle for a few weeks or months of fun.

Your list should also be the basis for your prayers

*And whatever things you ask in prayer, believing, you will receive. - Matthew 21:22 (NKJV)*

1. Pray over your list often. I am not going to tell you to pray the same thing every day or every week, etc. But pray as often as the desire for a mate pops in your head. It does not have to be a specific prayer or a specific scripture, but it does have to be sincere. I just break out my list and say "Thank you Lord for my husband, thank you that he is _____."

2. Pray for guidance. The word says that He is a lamp unto our feet. Pray that the Holy Spirit will guide you to be in the right place at the right time.

3. Pray for spiritual wisdom and discernment. That you may quickly discern who the right person is. Just because you want what you want, does not mean it will come in the package you want.
4. Pray for patience. Recognize that you are worth the wait and the journey toward marriage will take time. You should not want to rush into marriage nor should you want someone who wants to rush into marriage.
5. Pray for help. That you remain teachable and allow God to help you become the woman and wife He wants you to be. That all you desire in a mate is perfected in you as well.
6. Pray for peace. Rest in knowing that your prayers will be answered. Rest in knowing that God is not ignoring you. Rest in knowing that your husband is on the way.

Remember God gave us dominion over everything in the Earth except other people! The only person you can control is you. If you do your best and give your best, you will attract the best. Stop allowing the enemy to make you doubt God's plan for your life. If you desire marriage, God desires it for you...Period! God is an on time God, whenever your Mr. Right comes he will be right on time!

# Chapter 9
## Preparing for Marriage

*"Then the kingdom of heaven shall be likened to ten virgins who took their lamps and went out to meet the bridegroom. Now five of them were wise, and five were foolish. Those who were foolish took their lamps and took no oil with them, but the wise took oil in their vessels with their lamps.*
*And while they went to buy, the bridegroom came, and those who were ready went in with him to the wedding; and the door was shut. "Afterward the other virgins came also, saying, 'Lord, Lord, open to us!' But he answered and said, 'Assuredly, I say to you, I do not know you.' "Watch therefore, for you know neither the day nor the hour in which the Son of Man is coming.*
*Matthew 25: 1-4; 10-13 (NKJV)*

Wouldn't it be awful if your husband came and you were not ready? When he approached you, you were out of oil and thus you were unable to see him through the darkness? The oil refers to the word of God. Without the word you are not properly prepared for the blessings God has for you. How to prepare for marriage, is a question that only God can answer. It requires a customized answer. No two people are alike. But it is that journey towards wholeness and completeness in Him that is required to be truly prepared for marriage.

My previous book "Stop Asking Why Are You Single" as well as the previous eight chapters thus far have all been geared toward preparing for marriage. Since I cannot specifically say what all women should do to prepare for marriage, I can give insight into my personal journey:

**Allow God to heal you.** Many women like to believe they are the "perfect" or "good" woman. I do not dispute that fact. Everything God made was good and perfect. However to assume that you do not have issues is ridiculous. To constantly question your singleness....Is an issue! To not allow yourself to be happy because you don't have a man....Is an issue! To go from bad relationship to bad relationship, and not begin a self-analysis.....Is an issue! Singleness is a prerequisite of marriage. You can't skip it, so you might as well enjoy it. No man should be responsible for your happiness, happiness is within and comes from God. The common denominator in all your bad relationships is YOU, not him! Allow God to show you the root of your issues, and allow him to mend your brokenness. The longer you avoid it, the longer you will be miserable, and though singleness is not a curse, yes the longer you will be single. God will not bring anybody else into that mess.

**Allow God to show you who you are in Him.** Life without purpose is life devoid of joy and direction. The whole plan of the enemy is that you don't know who you are. Your past failures, past heartaches, current pain and present bitterness are all to keep you from the magnificent plan and abundant life God has for you. All those issues block you from your true identity. Because you lack identity you seek validation from someone else, a husband, a relationship, a title, etc. It is not healthy to covet what someone else has. It is not healthy to compare yourself to the lifestyles of others. You must learn to be happy and content right where God has you. The secret to contentment is found in identity. Purpose gives you purpose, without it you are still wondering around in the wilderness.

**Trust and Submit to God.** The word tells us that wives must submit to their husbands. Submission requires trust. God is the first man, authority figure that we must learn to submit to. The word also tells us that singles are to be concerned with pleasing the Lord. Therefore God is your husband, He is your provider, He is your stability, He is your shelter, and He is your security. He is all that you look for and require in a mate, if you allow Him to be. We have to learn to stop questioning God. Stop asking why we are single and stop entertaining people who question our singleness. Do you want the promise or do you want what's familiar and comfortable? Are you going to trust God, submit to his authority or do it your own way?

**Be willing to be hurt.** Are you ready to get rid of the fear of being hurt? Love, unconditional love, does not mean that it will not hurt. But it should not be intentional. Are you avoiding dating for fear of rejection or of being hurt? How else are you going to meet your Mr. Right? God is love. God loves us whether we mess up or not. In fact he knows we are not perfect. Every time we mess up, we hurt him, but He loves us anyway. Are you ready to love, even when you feel hurt?

**Get rid of materialistic expectations.** Looks, money, houses, and cars all fade or can vanish in the blink of the eye. Marriage is for life, better to marry someone you can be with for the long haul rather than have it based on things of diminishing value. Materialistic expectations block your spiritual vision. You will not be able to recognize who God has for you, if you are looking for a specific package.

**Patience.** Like I said earlier, marriage should not be taken lightly. Don't rush it. As women we spend so much time daydreaming and planning the wedding, we forget to put time and effort into the relationship. Patience is required before and especially after you say I do. You can't change him and he can't change you. You will need patience to allow God to do the changing in both of you.

**Sacrifice your needs for his.** In other words are you ready to get rid of your selfish ways. Joyce Meyers, in a marriage conference, spoke on 5 areas of sacrifice in marriage:

1. Personal desires – It is more blessed to give than to receive. The more you give, the more you will receive. You must be willing to relinquish your wants to make the other person happy.

2. Pride – You cannot demand to be right or self-seeking. You must be willing to be wrong even when you know you are right.

3. Touchiness - Get out of your feelings. If it bothers the other person, don't do it. Always opt to keep the peace.

4. Bitterness, resentment, and forgiveness – Don't be bitter or resent them for what they do or who they are. Leave the past in the past, forgive quickly, and move on.

5. Sex life – Don't reject him. Don't use sex as a weapon or bargaining tool. If you find yourself saying No more than you say yes, you leave room for the enemy to attack. Saying no to sex should only be done on rare occasions.

**Learn to communicate effectively**. Communication is perhaps the number one hindrance to a good marriage. Lack of communication and failure to communicate effectively can lead to many issues and even divorce. Talk about everything, including money, plans, reasons why you do or don't do things or regarding something you said or didn't say, children, your feelings or moods, etc. Lack of direct communication leaves an open place for suspicion. How do you handle anger? Don't discuss issues in the heat of emotions. Don't push the issue if either party is angry, walk away, take a breather, and tackle it later. Stay on subject, don't bring up past issues or failures. Avoid abusive, accusing, or over-exaggerated statements or words (like always and never). No one can read your mind, don't be vague or hint. Learning to communicate takes time. Practice makes perfect. I used to be easily offended (still working on it). But God showed me, that the source of my anger was that I didn't feel heard. I assumed people knew how I felt or presumed they understood me because they "knew" me. I learned to tell people how I felt. If I am in a bad mood, I say I'm not in a good mood. If I don't like what someone said or what they said made me feel a certain way, I say so. Not only does it make me feel heard, it makes me feel better, reduces the time I am angry or stressed, and eliminates the post-conversation thoughts of what I should have said or done.

**Be willing to share your life and have an accountability partner.** What is the point of getting married if you are going to still behave like you are single? If it repulses you to tell someone where you are going, when you will be back, discuss your spending or your daily plans, you may want to rethink this marriage thing. If you still want to hang out twice a week or take a quarterly trip with your girlfriends, what is the point of getting married? Not saying that time with friends is not important, but your independence should not supersede the becoming of one between you and your spouse. You cannot become one, if you still want to spend time alone or with others.

**Learn to manage your finances wisely.** Learn now to not overspend. Don't put added pressure on your husband by living beyond your means. Don't expect to be an instant stay at home wife, with a mountain of debt. You will have to work together to get finances straightened out, which means you will have to have some honest, hard conversations. Most importantly don't rob God, be a good steward and pay your tithes and offerings. Failure to do so could cause God's hand to be still in your marriage.

**Learn to manage your time wisely.** You must allow time for God, your spouse, and yourself. Yes in that order. Do something fruitful with your time. All your time should not be spent watching television or on social media. Wasting time is not productive. Pray daily asking God to show you what to do and how to spend your time wisely. Listen and make adjustments accordingly. This is very important as singles, because we assume we have a lot of extra time because we are single. I remember when God dealt with me about watching television too much. We have to be careful of what we allow into our spirits. While we may think that television is just entertainment, the negativity that it portrays does affect your view of reality. If you constantly watch shows with violence, poor relationships, infidelity, adultery, etc. you begin to think it is a norm.

**Get rid of negativity.** Stop talking negatively about men, marriage, and relationships. How can you say in one minute that you want to be married; yet the next minute proclaim there are no good men out there? The bible says our words are spirit and life. What you say affects your reality. Stop talking negatively about other marriages. We have all been guilty of stating how so and so's husband is a dog or how so and so is a horrible wife. Remember you are on the outside looking in, regardless of what you think you know, you only know half of it. Pray for them and keep your negative tongue off that Godly union. What God has joined together let no man put asunder. Marriage is difficult, you better hope somebody is praying for you rather than talking about you. Also you will need to encourage and uplift your spouse. Optimism goes a lot further than pessimism. You will have to boost his ego and make him feel important. We all need to be lifted and it does not make him weak for needing it or you weak for doing it.

**Learn to accept imperfection.** This one generally starts within. Once you can accept the imperfections in yourself, you are more willing and more acceptable of the imperfections in others. You must learn that your way is not the only way. This will be especially hard for Ms. Independent but unless you want to remain independent you must learn to let him lead and do things his own way and in his own time. You must learn to not compare your spouse to others. Not only is this the quickest way to an argument it is a straight road to divorce. Comparison tells the other person they are not good enough. Would you want to be married to someone who thinks you are beneath them? If there is something about the other person you don't like, voice it in love, and allow them to correct it in their own timing. Remember God changes people, not you.

**Remain teachable.** God is the ultimate guide and foundation for a good marriage. Remember God also uses people. Don't tell everything to everyone, but you both should have someone to talk to and to confide in that is neutral, respectful of your marriage, and has a high regard for confidentiality. As singles talk to other married couples or women. Don't refuse good advice, especially from those who have been married 10, 15, 20 plus years. However don't seek counsel from unsaved, ungodly folk. If you know Mrs. Jones is cheating on her husband, you don't need to ask her advice on how to prepare for marriage. The bible says we will know them by their fruits. You will know the right mentors you will need at the right time. Singles who desire marriage, tend to forget that they need to be mentored. If there are married women in your church, go out to lunch or dinner with them one day and take your note pad. You will be amazed at the willingness to share and the amount of wisdom that they will give.

**Discover your purpose**. An idle mind is the devils playground. Don't just sit around waiting for your Mr. Right to come along and take you on a journey of adventure and excitement. Get busy now. Not just any work but God's work. Pursue purpose. Learn to live in the moment. Enjoy life now. Discover your likes and dislikes now. If you don't know your purpose, you will get lost in his. Volunteer, travel, take a class, join a gym, etc.; don't be afraid to try new things. Rather than complaining about what you don't have, enjoy what you do have: time to explore you! Get active in church, your community, or your child's school; someone needs you now.

**Develop a relationship with God**. The ultimate guide to prepare for marriage is found in God. In loving Him we learn to love others. In obeying him we learn how to treat others. Learn to recognize his voice and quickly heed his instructions. The word is our foundation. If you put God on the back burner now, it will be difficult to go to him with confidence later. Marriage, as is our journey through life, is a continual changing process; we cannot expect the fullness of joy in those things without the creator.

**Get rid of sin.** God will not pour new wine into an old bottle. The word tells us that if we love him we keep his commandments. We cannot knowingly practice sin and expect God to bless us anyway. Yes this means, fornication. As singles we should not be indulging in sexual activity of any kind. Contrary to what the world thinks, your body will not explode, if you don't get any. Shacking is not a prerequisite of marriage, no matter what he says. You do not need to try before you buy. You must learn self-control. Since it is one of the fruits of the spirit, it is possible. Sex was created by God to produce fruit and to aid in the becoming of one in the confines of marriage. We cannot allow that which is Godly to be polluted by selfish gain, lustful desires, and reckless decisions. Your body is the temple of the Holy Spirit. Don't allow someone who is not your spouse to befoul your temple. We must get rid of not only sexual sin, but any sin. Sin separates us from God. Sin exemplifies that you are led by your flesh rather than the Spirit of God.

*A person without self-control is like a city without broken-down walls. - Proverbs 25:28 (NLT)*

Sin leaves one open to the attack of the enemy. Sin removes us from the protection of God. The Holy Spirit is there to guide us into all truths. He chastises us when we unknowingly mess up. But when we knowingly commit sin, doing what we know is wrong, just because we have free will and it makes us feel good, we grieve the Holy Spirit and are vulnerable to the enemy. Anything we desire of the Lord and from the Lord begins with obedience. God is faithful to those who obey his commands. Once you know better, better is required of you.

# Chapter 10
## A Closer Walk with Thee:
### Developing a Consistent Relationship with God

*I am the vine; you are the branches. He who abides in Me, and I in him, bears much fruit; for without Me you can do nothing. If anyone does not abide in Me, he is cast out as a branch and is withered away; and they gathered them and throw them into the fire, and they are burned. If you abide in Me, and My words abide in you, you will ask what you desire, and it shall be done for you. By this My Father is glorified, that you bear much fruit; so you will be My disciples.*
*John 15: 5 – 8 (NKJV)*

We are living in a world where Christianity is popular yet taken for granted. Many claim to be Christian yet their lifestyles reflect otherwise. The bible is used as a reference tool of convenience. Many use scriptures that benefit them but when the word conflicts with their behaviors, they ignore it. As long as all is right in their world, God is not needed, they are #livingitup, #turnedup, #singlelife, #winning or whatever catch phrase they use to express their happiness. But when things go wrong they wonder where is God, why He has forsaken them, or why do bad things happen to good people, etc., etc.

Christians are praising God one minute and the next minute using language so profane to express anger at their haters or whomever, followed by "don't judge me" or "pray for me." "God knows my heart" is a phrase used, over utilized in my opinion, to justify knowingly sinful behavior and an excuse to keep doing it. Sin is welcomed, as long as it makes you happy and you are not hurting anyone. Earthly pleasures override Godly principle.

Christians fear being labeled "holier than thou", "sanctified", or "judgmental" if they choose to live and portray a lifestyle against the norms of society. So they hide, conform, remain silent, or diminish their own values for a "politically correct", "tolerated", and "non-confrontational" existence. They choose a lifestyle on the fence, doing just enough to hopefully make it in on judgement day. They proclaim they are happy, blessed, highly favored, and waiting on their season of reaping. On Sunday, they are fire baptized, Holy Ghost filled, bible toting, praise dancing, prayer warriors, tongue talking Saints sold-out for Jesus, but Monday thru Saturday they are cussing, gossiping, lying, stealing, cheating, doubting, faith-lacking, fearful hypocrites. Let's not forget the Pseudo-Saints. In church every time the doors swing open: Sunday school, Sunday morning service, Sunday evening service, bible study, prayer meeting, choir practice, usher board meeting, etc., but they have yet to step out on faith, or they have no time for God in between work, school, church, home, and activities.

Is God pleased? Is this the lifestyle he came for, suffered for, died for, and rose for? Does he want our lives and relationships to have an on again off again, start and stop, connotation?

*These people draw near to Me with their mouth, and honor Me with their lips, but their heart is far from Me. And in vain they worship Me, teaching as doctrine the commandments of men. - Matthew 15: 8-9 (NKJV)*

God wants your heart! Many people believe Christianity begins and ends with the Cross, implying that believing that Jesus was the son of God and died for our sins is enough. However that is just the beginning, it is what happens after the AMEN that is equally, if not more important.

What's your salvation story? Many quote the day they walked down the aisle in tears and recited the prayer to receive Christ or the day they were baptized. But go deeper. Your salvation story should consist of the day or moment, it all made sense, you changed your ways and followed Christ. If the sinners prayer was not followed by transformation, if you just wiped your eyes, went back to your seat, went back to your home, and back to your old life, then you are missing the best part of salvation. True repentance means to ask for forgiveness and turn from. If things stayed the same, then you have yet to accept Christ as your Lord and Savior.

True salvation is exemplified in our lifestyle, our expression of our love for him and our willingness to accept his ways for our ways. In reward, He has promised us the keys to the kingdom. He has promised us the desires of our hearts and His love perfected in us.

*Now by this we know that we know Him, if we keep His commandments. He who says, "I know Him," and does not keep His commandments, is a liar, and the truth is not in him. But whosoever keeps His word, truly the love of God is perfected in Him. By this we know that we are in Him. He who says he abides in Him ought himself also to walk just as He walked. - 1 John 2: 3-6 (NKJV)*

How do we abide in Him? Go back to the beginning.
*In the beginning was the Word, and the Word was with God, and the Word was God. - John 1: 1 (NKJV)*

It begins with the word. After the prayer and the benediction, we need the word daily. We cannot continue to call ourselves Christians, yet put the word on the back burner. Going to church is not enough, we must know God for ourselves. We manage to find time and fit everything else in our schedule; we have to do the same for God. In fact, schedule Him in until it becomes habit. Here are a few tips to help you get started:

1. The bible on CD. Listen to the word in your car, on the way to where ever, when you awake as you get ready for work, etc. Though it may seem like you are not paying attention, it is sinking it. You could even listen at night, while you sleep. The Spirit Man never slumbers.
2. Get up 15 minutes early. Even a few minutes reading the word is helpful.
3. Go to bed 15 minutes late. Read until you fall asleep. For some reason the bible seems to be the cure for insomnia. Go figure!
4. Read a few verses on your break at work.
5. Bring your lunch and drive to the park for quiet time with the Lord
6. If you have the option of listening to music while you work or work out, listen to the bible CD instead.
7. Sermon podcasts. If you prefer to hear a message.
8. Bible apps on your phone. Many apps make it possible to listen and read the bible at your convenience. They even have daily reading plans that they can send you reminders for.
9. Cut off the TV or radio. Replace them with reading the word and/or listening to inspirational music
10. Eliminate social media. Again replace Facebook, twitter, Instagram, etc. with reading the word and/or listening to inspirational music.

It's not really as hard as people think. It's just not their idea of fun. I challenge you to take a few days and analyze your time. Print out a daily planner page from online. With each hour of the day indicated, record your activities for that hour. Then notice how much time you spent doing things other than sleeping. Pay close attention to idle time watching television, talking on the phone, meaningless conversations at work, social media, games, stuck in traffic, etc.

Poor time management is the number one trick of the enemy to keep us from spending time in the word. God not only speaks to us IN His word, He speaks THROUGH His word. In the bible we find the answers to the issues of life. Through the word the Holy Spirit guides us into all truths, gives us daily direction, and explicit instruction. The word calms our flesh and gives us peace. It is extremely hard to be angry while reading the word.

In times of trouble, the Holy Spirit brings the word back to our remembrance. If we don't put any word in, the Holy Spirit has nothing to bring back. There will come a time when the bible will not be as accessible as it is today. Though you may feel the natural man is not taking it all in, the Spirit Man is hiding it in your heart. Bottom line, quit making excuses. We must on purpose spend time in the word. Sacrifice time, other activities, and even other people for time in the word.

**Spend time praying.**

Praying is our communication with God. It is how we speak with Him and how He speaks with us. I never understood how some people can claim to be so holy yet don't know how to pray. There is no right or wrong way to pray. Stop thinking that you have to pray like your pastor, church mother, deacon, evangelist, prophet or prophetess. Title does not matter, all that is required is that you speak from the heart.

Jesus' death on the cross gave us all direct access to the Father. Therefore, you don't need anybody else to pray for you. Plus you don't want to leave your fate in someone else's hand. What if you ask Evangelist so and so to pray for you and she forgets? What if they are having a bad day and don't feel like praying and just touch you on the forward head saying "fix it Jesus." Don't nobody know like you know and can't nobody tell it like you can tell it.

If you are honest, the truth is not that you can't pray. The problem is you don't really feel like you can get a prayer through. Your sin is blocking you. You know you are not perfect so you don't feel comfortable praying. Well Evangelist so and so ain't perfect either. None of us are. Repent and restore your relationship with God and get back to your prayer life.

Perhaps you feel like your prayers have become redundant. Are you asking for and praying for the same thing over and over? Guess what? So what, God wants us to be persistent. If it is truly what you want then keep asking and praying. However I have felt the same way that my prayers were empty. I now know this is a trick of the enemy, to keep you from praying at all. But here are a few tips:

1. Pray using scriptures. Find a verse or two that coincides with your need. This is actually how God wants us to pray.
2. Pray for others. We can run out of things to say for ourselves but have plenty to say for others. Remember the word says what you do for others, God will make happen for you. I believe God sends others to us for this very reason.
3. Don't ask for anything at all, just worship and reverence Him. Spend time saying thank you Lord for what He has done and for what He is going to do. Praise moves God.
4. Pray in tongues. While we may be speechless at times, the spirit man always knows what to say. If you don't speak in tongues, ask God to give it to you. Call upon the elders of your church to pray with you to receive the baptismal of the Holy Ghost with evidence of speaking in tongues.
5. Sit in silence. Sit in His presence to hear from Him. This will require practice. Your mind will try to wonder.
6. Start by reading scripture. If you are having an issue, look in the concordance or "help" section, find specific scriptures for your issue and read those verses out loud to begin your prayer. There is a book entitled "God's Promises & Answers For Your Life," that is amazing we you need an answer quick!

*But you, when you pray, go into your room, and when you have shut your door, pray to your Father who is in the secret place; and your Father who sees in secret will reward you openly. –Matthew 6:6 (NKJV)*

Again God always gives a reward for His commands. How can we expect an open reward before we pray as required in secret? Start now. Stop making excuses. Praying does not require a set time, a set language, or a set tone of voice. But it does require a righteous life style. As I stated earlier, you must live according to Godly principles, otherwise as the Saints of old say "your prayers won't go further than the ceiling." If sin is hindering your prayer, the good news is you can get it right.

**Learn to hear and heed God's voice.**

Once you have adapted consistency in reading the word and praying, God will speak. God speaks in a still, quiet voice. You have to get quiet to hear him. Quiet your thoughts, quiet your surroundings, and tune in to His grace, mercy, and kindness. The key to hearing God is to get in His presence. God's presence is anywhere an atmosphere of worship is created. Which means it can be your car, your house, at church, etc.

*Finally, brethren, whatever things are true, whatever things are noble, whatever things are just, whatever things are pure, whatever things are lovely, whatever things are of good report, if there is any virtue and if there is anything praiseworthy – meditate on these things. The things which you learned and received and heard and saw in me, these do, and the God of peace will be with you.*
- Philippians 4: 8 – 9 (NKJV)

To enter into God's presence begins with quieting your thoughts. The mind is always going so you have to give it something good to think about. It basically means to lay your issues, concerns, wants, and needs aside and praise God anyhow. It's difficult to think about your now issues when you know what God has done in the past. This is how we get to know God. We learn of His goodness and faithfulness through our trials and tribulations. If He has done it before, he can do it again.

Getting into His presence can be a little different for some of us. I meditate and clear my mind while listening to music. I also hear him clearly when I am writing. I am at the greatest peace when I am writing. I used to think of writing as a hobby, or something to do to earn a living in the future. But God showed me that when I write I am in direct communion with Him.

Now I understand why the push to write is so strong and the conviction when I go days and weeks without writing is as equally strong.

The more time you spend in His presence, the more you will crave it. The peace and joy that results is priceless and well worth the time. Think about it, when we meet a new beau, we know that we have to spend quality time with them and daily communication to get to know them. We must tackle our relationship with God the same way. The more we know him, the more His thoughts become our thoughts and the more His ways become our ways.

If you are still confused about your purpose, what God has for you, whether marriage is God's desire for you, or any question you have before the Lord; the confusion is indication that your relationship is lacking.

*He answered and said to them, "Because it has been given to you to know the mysteries of the kingdom of heaven, but to them it has not been given. - Matthew 13:11 (NKJV)*

God does not withhold answers from his children. Confusion is not of God, it is a trick of the enemy to produce doubt and keep you stagnant. You don't have to wonder what God's will is for your life, all you have to do is ask. Then patiently wait for His response. How does God speak?

1. Through His word. The Holy Spirit will guide you to a specific scripture, or perhaps you will hear a message that speaks directly to your issues, such as in Church.
2. Through dreams. Have you ever awakened from a dream that you couldn't get out of your mind? Perhaps the Lord is trying to tell you something. Pray that He reveal the meaning of the dream to you. Or go to someone with the gift of dream interpretation.
3. Through others. Prophets, Prophetess', and even strangers can often relay a message from the Lord to you. Generally the word comes as confirmation to what God may have already spoken.

4. Small still voice. Many call this intuition, or use the phrase "something told me." Since the Holy Spirit lives in me, that something has a name, and His name is the Holy Ghost
5. Through prayer. Have you ever been praying or speaking in tongue and got a strong inclination to say or do something? Or perhaps got a vision of a person or thing to pray for.

You will know that it is NOT God if it:
1. Goes against the word of God. God will NEVER go against His word. The word of God will never take you where the grace of God cannot protect you.
2. It will bring harm or hurt to others. God will not bless someone by bringing hurt to someone else. Ex: A woman waiting for her boyfriend to get divorced to marry her! God will not give you someone else's husband. That is adultery and therefore against His word.

God created us to commune with Him. Failure to do so is why our lives are in turmoil and we are not basking in His promises. Please don't misunderstand, along with that communication, faith and patience is also needed. God did not promise instant manifestation, nor did he promise life without trials and trouble. Remember that in order to get to the promise land we have to go through the wilderness.

The significance of relationship with God is so that our faith and confidence in Him is unwavering. If we keep our mind stayed on Him, He promises to keep us in perfect peace. It is His peace that gives us strength and comfort in knowing that what He promised, He is faithful to perform. While salvation is free to all, it is the working of that salvation that requires sacrifice. Trust Him and know that the promise is on the way and whenever it comes, it will be right on time. Don't allow the cares or the expectations of the world to cause you to doubt God. Know that God loves you. Allow Him to complete a work in you. Relax and enjoy the journey. Remember

God is time. Therefore time will not run out before His promises are fulfilled.

www.ingramcontent.com/pod-product-compliance
Lightning Source LLC
Chambersburg PA
CBHW021132300426
44113CB00006B/395